Expertise

KEYWORDS IN TEACHER EDUCATION

Series Editor: Viv Ellis

Taking cultural theorist Raymond Williams's concept as an organizing device, the **Keywords in Teacher Education** series offers short, accessibly written books on the most pressing and challenging ideas in the field.

Teacher education has a high profile in public policy and professional debates given the enduring associations between how teachers are prepared and how well their students do in school. At the same time, research perspectives on the important topics in the field are increasingly polarized with important consequences for the kind of teacher and the qualities of teaching that are most valued. Written by internationally recognized experts, these titles offer analyses both of the historical emergence and the consequences of the different positions in these debates.

Forthcoming in the series:

Communities, Ken Zeichner
Identity, Sarah Steadman
Quality, Clare Brooks
Disadvantage, Jo Lampert, Jane Wilkinson, Mervi Kaukko and Rocío García-Carrión
Knowledge, Steven Puttick, Victoria Elliott and Jenni Ingram

Expertise

JESSICA GERRARD AND JESSICA HOLLOWAY

BLOOMSBURY ACADEMIC
LONDON • NEW YORK • OXFORD • NEW DELHI • SYDNEY

BLOOMSBURY ACADEMIC
Bloomsbury Publishing Plc
50 Bedford Square, London, WC1B 3DP, UK
1385 Broadway, New York, NY 10018, USA
29 Earlsfort Terrace, Dublin 2, Ireland

BLOOMSBURY, BLOOMSBURY ACADEMIC and the Diana logo are
trademarks of Bloomsbury Publishing Plc

First published in Great Britain 2023

Cover design by Charlotte James
Cover image © Zoonar GmbH / Alamy Stock Photo

A catalogue record for this book is available from the British Library.

A catalog record for this book is available from the Library of Congress.

ISBN: HB: 978-1-3502-3823-7
         PB: 978-1-3502-3822-0
         ePDF: 978-1-3502-3825-1
         eBook: 978-1-3502-3824-4

Series: Keywords in Teacher Education

Typeset by Integra Software Services Pvt. Ltd.
Printed and bound in Great Britain

To find out more about our authors and books visit www.bloomsbury.com
and sign up for our newsletters.

CONTENTS

SERIES EDITOR'S FOREWORD

This series is organized by the concept of 'keywords', first elaborated by Welsh cultural theorist Raymond Williams (1976), and books in the series will seek to problematize and unsettle the ostensibly unproblematic and settled vocabulary of teacher education. From Williams's perspective, keywords are words and phrases that occur frequently in speech and writing, allowing conversation to ensue, but that nonetheless reveal profound differences in meaning within and across cultures, politics and histories. In teacher education, such keywords include practice, knowledge, quality and expertise. The analysis of such keywords allows us to trace the evolution of the emergent – and the maintenance of residual – meanings in teacher education discourses and practices. By analysing keywords, therefore, it is possible to elucidate the range of meanings of what Gallie (1955) referred to as 'essentially contested concepts', but in ways that promote a critical, historical understanding of changes in the fields in which they occur.

In the first edition of *Keywords*, Williams included entries on 108 units, ranging from 'Aesthetic' to 'Work'. A second edition followed in 1983 and other writers have subsequently used the concept to expand on Williams's original collection (e.g. Bennett et al, 2005; MacCabe & Yanacek, 2018) or to apply the concept to specific domains (e.g. A Community of Inquiry, 2018). This series applies it to teacher education. The purpose of the series mirrors that of Williams's original project: to trace ideological differences and social conflicts over time as they relate to the discourses and practices of a field (here, teacher education) by focusing on a selection of the field's high-frequency words. So Keywords in Teacher Education is not a multi-volume dictionary. Each book will explore a critically important issue in teacher education by interrogating one significant lexical item in its vocabulary.

The kind of analysis required by a focus on keywords goes beyond etymology or historical semantics. By selecting and analysing keywords, Williams argued:

> we find a history and complexity of meanings; conscious changes, or consciously different uses; innovation, obsolescence, specialization, extension, overlap, transfer; or changes which are masked by a nominal continuity so that words which seem to have been there for centuries, with continuous general meanings, have come in fact to express radically different or radically variable, yet sometimes hardly noticed, meanings and implications of meaning.
>
> (Williams, 1976, p 17)

Given the increasingly strong attention given to teacher education in education policy and in public debates about education more generally, focusing on keywords in this field is both timely and necessary. Uncovering and unsettling differences and conflicts in the vocabulary of preparing teachers renders the political and social bases underlying policy formation and public discourse more visible and therefore more capable of being acted upon.

Through this organizing device, the Keywords in Teacher Education series addresses the most important topics and questions in teacher education currently. It is a series of short books written in a direct and accessible style, each book taking one keyword as its point of departure and closely examining its cultural meanings historically while, crucially, identifying the social force and material consequences of the differences and conflicts in meaning. Written by internationally recognized researchers, each peer-reviewed book offers cutting-edge analysis of the keyword underpinned by a deep knowledge of the available research within the field – and beyond it. One of the aims of the series is to broaden the gaze of teacher education research by engaging more systematically with the relevant humanities and social science literature – to acknowledge, as Williams did, that our understanding is deepened and potential for action strengthened by seeking to understand the social relations between words, texts and the multiple contexts in which their meanings are produced.

In this first volume in the series, Jessica Gerrard and Jessica Holloway take expertise as our opening keyword. Expertise – particularly as in 'teacher expertise' – is undoubtedly a high-frequency word in the vocabulary of neoliberal teacher education reform, where it is often collocated with quality (as in 'teaching quality') and channelled through the discourse of influential psychological theories of expertise, such as those of K. Anders Ericsson (e.g. Ericsson et al, 1993). Ericsson's concept of 'deliberate practice' has become commonplace in the teacher education lexicon, inspired by the relatively optimistic assumption that anyone can learn to teach; it just takes practice. But also that what you're learning (teaching) has a pre-defined and universally agreed end point (teacher expertise becoming encoded in competences or standards).

Equally, expertise has been a frequent feature of professionalizing discourses in the history of teacher education – teachers' individual or collective repertoire of beliefs, sayings and doings – expertise constituting their claim to professional status in a changing economic and labour relations landscape. This way of using expertise is one that has been challenged in recent years by populist authoritarians in governments around the world who have declared that 'we' (meaning they) 'have had enough of experts'. Gerrard and Holloway trace these relations between knowledge, authority, objectivity, data, governance (who is governed and how, by experts) and other dimensions of what are ultimately political questions of hegemonic social formations. The authors conclude that, rather than seeking to evacuate politics from education, teachers need to 'get political'. Gerrard and Holloway's *Expertise* is a brilliant first volume in the series and one that also extends the discussion of keywords and other aspects of Williams's theories.

Viv Ellis
Melbourne, 2022

References

A Community of Inquiry (2018). *Keywords; for Further Consideration and Particularly Relevant to Academic Life, Especially as It Concerns Disciplines, Inter-Disciplinary Endeavor and Modes of Resistance to the Same.* Princeton, NJ: Princeton University Press.

Bennett, T., Grossberg, L., & Morris, M. (2005). *New Keywords. A Revised Vocabulary of Culture and Society.* Oxford: Blackwell Publishing.

Ericsson, K. A., Krampe, R. T., & Tesch-Romer, C. (1993). The role of deliberate practice in the acquisition of expert performance. *Psychological Review, 100*(3), 363–406.

Gallie, W. B. (1955). Essentially contested concepts. *Proceedings of the Aristotelian Society, 56,* 167–98.

McCabe, C., Yanacek, H., & the Keywords Project. (2018). *Keywords for Today. A 21st Century Vocabulary.* Oxford: Oxford University Press.

Williams, R. (1976). *Keywords: A Vocabulary of Culture and Society.* London, UK: Fontana.

ACKNOWLEDGEMENTS

Writing always involves the company of others. It always involves thinking with, thinking through and sometimes thinking against others' ideas. This book would not have been possible without the faithful colleagues who have written before us and who have inspired many of our thoughts in these pages. Similarly, collaboration – thankfully – is also sometimes more explicitly woven into the act of writing itself, as is the case here. This book – written over the course of two years – is the product of many conversations between us, as well as constant revisits to the classics and contemporaries that stimulated our ever-evolving ideas. Through this process, we found generative common ground across our own research agendas and – we hope – have forged something new.

As such, we are indebted to the community of scholars – both those who we know in real life and those who we just know on the page – whose work supports, challenges and provokes us.

We are particularly grateful for the careful, generous and constructive feedback of Meg Maguire, Nicole Mockler, Chris Speldewinde and the Bloomsbury anonymous reviewer on earlier drafts. It's in these moments of collegiate generosity that we are reminded of the importance of (and are indebted to) intellectual community, care and the willingness to share expertise.

Thanks too must go to Viv Ellis – series editor – and Anna Elliss, Alison Baker and colleagues at Bloomsbury for supporting the manuscript and patiently awaiting its arrival as we juggled Covid-19 lockdowns, work and life over the course of this project.

Finally, we would be remiss not to mention our truly enduring champions.

Jessica Gerrard would like to thank Manda, Indigo and Aster for their unflappable enthusiasm for dancing around the living room. Jessica Holloway would like to thank Steven for his endless supply of encouragement, laughs and coffee. She would also like to thank her dad, who passed midway through writing this, but who nonetheless cheered us on until the end.

This work was supported in part by the Australian Research Council (grant number DE190101140: Jessica Holloway).

CHAPTER ONE

'Expertise' as Keyword

In his original conception of 'keywords', Raymond Williams (1985) addresses the power, the *force*, of vocabulary. Recounting his experience as a working-class student at England's elite and prestigious Cambridge University, and then his return to England from armed service some six years later, Williams notes a sense of being out-of-place emerging from the reflection that 'they just don't speak the same language' (1985, p 12). These experiences led Williams to an inquiry into language – and in particular vocabulary – to explore how words shape our understanding of the world, including creating and confirming taken-for-granted ways of understanding and being. Particularly intrigued by the emerging significance of the word 'culture', the outcome of his inquiry was the highly influential book, *Keywords: A Vocabulary of Society and Culture* (1985 [originally published in 1976]). The approach of *Keywords* was to identify significant terms, or what he referred to as 'binding words' (Williams, 1985, p 15), that are windows into the ways culture and society are understood, shaped and expressed. That is, the words identified in *Keywords* by Williams are a means by which to understand the problematic of 'culture' and 'society' (and related significant words) as concepts that are not – and cannot be – simplistic reflections of 'reality' out there, but which shape what we even understand 'reality' to be.

When it comes to the field of education, 'expertise' is undoubtedly a keyword. It has rising significance and power in policy and practice, yet what it means is diversely interpreted and contested. It is also far more complex a term than straightforwardly describing a stable set of practices or processes. Yet not only is the meaning of expertise essentially contested, it also has force. What this means is that to use the terms 'expertise' and 'experts' in relation to teachers *does* something; it shapes how we understand the work of teachers, their relationship to students and the community, and the role of teachers in society. In the current moment, debates abound regarding the need for more teacher expertise, different teacher expertise or more respect for teacher expertise. Expertise is central to public debates and policy contestations, from those about teacher professionalism to the exercise of professional judgement, the kinds of knowledge that gets taught in school, and the authority of teachers' understanding of students' learning. A central premise of this book is that these kinds of debates cannot be resolved by a more refined definition of expertise. By viewing (teacher) expertise as a keyword in the spirit of Raymond Williams's approach, we see these debates as perennial and symbolic of the deep social, cultural, political and economic relations that are brought to bear in any assertion of, claim to, defence of or rejection of expertise.

'Teacher expertise', therefore, signals deep claims about the purpose of schooling; the relationship between schooling to society and between students, parents and educators; and the value and merit of particular forms of knowledge in education. These kinds of claims are not steadfast, but are shifting, contested and socially contextualized; it is these that form the basis of this book. When we saw the call for proposals for this book series, we immediately saw a way for us to consolidate and develop an ongoing conversation between the two of us about the uses and meanings of expertise in teacher education. This book is not about identifying 'good' expertise or defining a set of teaching practices that might be labelled expert approaches. Rather, it is about reckoning with the force of the term 'expertise' in the context of teaching and teacher education. To paraphrase Williams, this does not purport to be a neutral investigation of expertise (indeed, we think that such neutrality is impossible); this book is an examination of the historical and social conditions that make expertise – a term with associated judgements surrounding practice, policies and meanings – so central to our understanding of teaching and schooling.

In this book, we make the case that expertise is constructed, always 'dangerous' and always something to be critiqued. We use 'danger' here in the sense that political philosopher Michel Foucault (1983) used it: not to suggest that something is necessarily bad, but to denote the underlying ethical and political dimensions that contour what might seem self-evident or unproblematic. As such, this book can be understood as an examination of an underpinning tension in teacher expertise: its ambivalence. Of course, distrust in teaching and teachers is often used to problematic political and educational ends. For instance, the political seeds of doubt about teachers are often used to justify further government or market-based intervention in education in the context of long-standing 'culture wars', whereby teachers are cast as dangerous progressives damaging children with child-centred, anti-standards, anti-racist, anti-sexist, anti-homophobic and trans-affirming learning communities (see Gerrard, 2020). At the same time, however, we think it's important not to ignore the ways claims to teacher expertise have also been used to problematic and sometimes violent ends, a part of intensive social dynamics that work *against* justice, recognition and equity.

It must be stated upfront that this book was difficult to write. All books are hard to write, of course, but there is something quite confronting about establishing oneself as an expert, while simultaneously filling a book with illustrations of why expertise is dangerous and sometimes deeply problematic. In the process of writing, oftentimes it was difficult to commit to words that are, in so many ways, troubling. This is compounded by the fact that we are two white women with secure employment, and at supportive, top-ranking universities. We cannot escape the fact that our privileged positions invariably shape our lens of expertise, as we have been fortunate enough to be recognized by institutional norms, practices and infrastructures that authorize us as experts. We didn't have to learn a second language to publish in international journals. Our onto-epistemic orientations are accepted within the academy (for the most part). And, we do not face the ongoing, racial injustices that our Black and brown colleagues confront every day. This does not mean that we are without our own challenges, of course, but it is important for us to think critically about who we are and how our expertise has been legitimized through channels that do not operate neutrally.

At its core, this is what this book is about. Using teacher expertise as a case in point, it takes expertise as a construct that should be understood within the political, social and historical conditions that authorize it. We ask questions such as: who is an expert in education and who gets to decide that? What is teacher expertise, and what channels have been put in place to legitimize and reward certain types of teacher expertise? We want to emphasize our view that we see expertise (and the expert) as objects of interrogation, with teacher education as a critical site for doing so. We start with this assumption because it allows us to think about teachers as subjects of expert practices and discourses, rather than simply human actors who should or should not be accepted as experts. Simultaneously, we see teacher education – defined as the channels through which such expertise is constructed, cultivated and certified – as also in need of scrutiny. We should note that when we say 'teacher education', we are referring specifically to formal ways that teachers are educated, such as through university-based programs, professional development and the like. However, we also acknowledge that education can mean something much broader to encompass the informal interactions and experiences that contribute to teachers' development as experts.

Thus, this book will not weigh in on the ongoing debate of whether teachers are experts (or should be viewed as such). Rather, we seek to go underneath the surface of this debate to consider why the expert status of teachers is so foundational to contemporary public, policy and scholarly debates in education. In fact, we think the current terms of the teacher-as-expert debate oversimplifies the issue of teacher expertise as an either/or question, rather than one that is about how, who and to what ends is expertise constructed over time, within a particular set of political, social, economic and discursive conditions. Thus, it is with these starting assumptions that we develop our argument over the course of the book. In doing so, we continually return to these questions regarding what is expertise, who counts as an expert and how are these matters decided and authorized? This will take us down a number of paths, including the historical and political construction of teacher expertise, the evolution of expertise over time, the relationship between experts and their communities and that between expertise and ignorance, the 'official' means of authorizing teacher expertise (e.g. accreditation, certification, licensing, etc.), the use of data, metrics and digital platforms in relation to teacher expertise, and how teacher expertise both governs and is governed.

Throughout the chapters, we will continue to centre the political as a critical dimension of expertise (and teacher expertise) by challenging the common assumptions that are often taken for granted. In doing so, we demonstrate that teacher expertise is embroiled in the social relations of power *and* is unavoidably political in its expression. Each chapter that follows, therefore, is building to our conclusion in which we suggest that 'getting political' is not just an inevitable part of teacher expertise, but a necessary basis of a claim to it. Across the book, we construct our argument by weaving through various vignettes – from our own experiences and research, as well as those depicted in secondary sources – to illustrate the complexity of defining, shaping and exercising expertise. In doing so, we aim to (1) paint a picture that challenges our collective urge to just 'listen to the experts', but also (2) bring new insights into how expertise – and in particular teacher expertise – is constituted as a means for governing societies. Again, with teacher expertise as our main focus, we will look specifically at how the teacher subject has been constituted in relation to expertise, while arguing that more nuanced understandings of expertise might help us secure schooling as a more just and critically responsive institution. We hope that teacher educators, as well as others from the fields of education, sociology and policy, will find these arguments useful.

Overview of the Book

In the following five chapters we address the tensions of teacher expertise as a cultural and social practice, mediated by power relations of the teaching profession, the state and of society more widely. To do so we elucidate four key themes related to the articulation of expertise in relation to teachers and teaching: society, expert/non-expert relationship, governance, and data and knowledge, before concluding with a reflection on the role of politics in teacher expertise.

The book starts by placing teacher expertise in historical and social context. In Chapter 2, 'Society, Teachers and Expertise', we explore how teacher expertise is socially constructed, is contested and is dependent on the function of institutions (schools, governments, universities), global/local relations and the social relations of the day. The chapter highlights key tensions in the past and present practice of teacher expertise, particularly surrounding the exercise of 'objectivity' in relation to understanding the human condition. Here, drawing on examples from research, we unpack how the so-called objectivity of experts has at times reproduced social inequalities by reflecting and deepening presumptions surrounding, for instance, differential intellectual ability based on the construction of race. In other words, expertise is inherently entangled within the social relations of power, framed by the past and present practices of colonialism and capitalism.

In Chapter 3, 'Challenging Expertise, Ignorance and the Un/known', we further examine the expression of these relations of power in an often-overlooked aspect of teacher expertise: how expertise is always constructed in relation to who its subjects are. Drawing on recent advances in 'ignorance studies', alongside current educational research, this chapter demonstrates: first, that expert knowledge is dynamically constituted through a constantly shifting boundary between the known and unknown (and what is understood or thought to be known and unknown); and second, that teacher expertise rests upon a relation between the expert and the so-called layperson or non-expert. This chapter therefore addresses key contemporary issues surrounding the exercise of student and parental agency over education. We argue that these relational dynamics of expertise (experts/non-experts, knowing/not knowing) are amplified in the case of teachers given the convergence of vested interests in schools and schooling, from parents, to the state, teachers, students, educational experts, teacher educators and even private agencies (such as corporations and philanthropies). We suggest that teacher expertise is often asserted via experiential and embodied means: to have expertise in education is to be (or to have been) a teacher. This raises important questions surrounding the boundaries of teacher expertise in relation to others with significant interest in – and claim to – school education.

Chapter 4, 'Governing Expertise', brings focused attention to the multiple investments and interests in education by exploring the relationship between expertise, authority and governance. We argue that new actors and discourses are shifting the modes through which teacher expertise is authorized, as well as who is involved in setting education policies, agendas and goals. What is often traditionally considered to be subject to a professional body's discretion and responsibility, such as licensure, standards and certification – has long attracted multiple vested interests and influences outside of the profession when it comes to teachers (and schooling more generally). In the current day, external bodies and key (state and non-state) actors play significant roles in writing policy, setting standards, providing curriculum materials and establishing accreditation criteria for teacher education. At the same time, however, we also invite readers to consider how institutions empowered to deliver teacher education (such as universities) also govern expertise.

In Chapter 5, 'Data, Knowledge and Expertise', we build from the previous chapters about the relational dimensions of teacher expertise to delve into the specific types of knowledge that have featured prominently in the construction of teacher expertise. We look historically at how metrics and quantification have gradually remade expertise, as a means for governing teachers and their practice, as well as establishing what teachers are meant to know. Drawing on some of our discussion from previous chapters about how expertise is formed and authorized in institutions (like teacher education), incentivized in the field (like with teacher appraisal systems) and normalized over time, the historical examination of metrics and numbers helps us see just how onto-epistemically powerful the datafication discourse has become. Specifically, we focus on two disciplines that have had profound influence on contemporary meanings and practices of teacher expertise: economics and data science. We conclude the chapter arguing that the 'datafication' of teachers is an attempt to neutralize expertise and requires a political, rather than a technical, response.

Finally, in Chapter 6, 'The Politics of Expertise', we bring together the themes of the book – society, the expert/non-expert relation, governance and data and knowledge – to argue the inevitability and importance of politics for teacher expertise. We contend that politics is the key element that articulates, animates and contests teacher expertise, which is ultimately what threads the arguments of this book together. That is, we implore readers to *get political*, rather than succumb to calls to get politics out of schools. As policy makers around the world craft legislation to notionally limit teachers' political influence on students (e.g. the 'Don't say gay bill' in Florida; legislative pushes to ban the *1619 Project* in US schools, Schwartz, 2021), we argue that teaching is never neutral and any attempt to treat teacher expertise as apolitical is disingenuous at best, and patently destructive at worst. Considering initial teacher education as one of the most important sites within which teacher expertise is made – the first induction into the profession of teaching – we conclude that there is one foundational antinomy that underscores the practice of teacher expertise: expertise governs and is governed.

CHAPTER TWO

Society, Teachers and Expertise

We start this chapter with two reflections from Indigenous teacher trainees – Curtis and Leanne – from a recent study in Canada on 'covert racism' in teacher education (Marom, 2019). These excerpts offer a powerful window into how the contemporary practice of teacher education – and the teaching profession itself – is steeped in social relations.

> In the practicum I did an activity … about residential schools and the children didn't know much about it. So I started by explaining these things, and my SA [School Advisor] pulled me aside and was like: 'you think that you can come here and teach just Native things? What Prescribed Learning Outcomes does it fit? Why are you teaching this?' And she added, 'you can tell that kids are bored with what you're teaching'.
>
> (Curtis in Marom, 2019, p 11)

> It is almost like you have to look like them, walk like them, dress like them, ask questions like them … There is an icon out there of what a teacher is supposed to look like, and how a teacher is supposed to behave … It's kind of a hidden protocol … If [one] fits this, [one] doesn't feel the pressure

of not being it, but the person who [doesn't fit], feels a subtle
pressure ... It would somehow be conveyed.
(Leanne in Marom, 2019, pp 7–8)

Curtis and Leanne's reflections point to core tensions in
the teaching profession surrounding schooling knowledge,
professional identity and authority, expertise, power and
Indigeneity. Their specific experiences reflect much broader
realities of the teaching profession and education: just like
schools, the teaching profession cannot escape the social
relations of marginality, exclusion and inequality. In this case,
the teaching of 'Native things' is brought into contestation with
'prescribed learning outcomes' and presumptions about what
'kids are bored with', and professional conduct and aesthetics
is mediated by an exclusionary 'hidden protocol'. Here,
Indigenous knowledge, identity and experience is marginalized
and minimized through a so-called professional commitment
to stipulated outcomes, notions of student interest and the
codification of professional conduct through particular
cultural and social norms, or what Indigenous Pueblo scholar
Calderon (2014) calls 'settler grammars' (see also Moodie &
Patrick, 2017).

Curtis and Leanne's experiences pry open the relationship
between teacher expertise and society. This relationship is the
foundation upon which teacher expertise – like all forms of
expertise – is developed, expressed, lived and felt. To put it
simply, experts – and expertise – shape society and are shaped
by it. Teacher expertise, as with all expertise, is a historically
and socially determined practice. Its production and enactment
cannot be separated from the social, political and cultural
meanings and practices of expertise, linked to codified practices
of professional judgement and authority. For instance, and
furthering our opening reflection about Curtis and Leanne and
the marginalization of Indigenous experiences in the teaching
profession, Indigenous Gomeroi/Gamilaraay scholar Nikki
Moodie's and colleague Rachel Patrick's (2017) analysis of
Australian teacher professional standards reveals that even

the 'recognition' and 'naming' of Indigenous perspectives (as is the case in the Australian standards) can become a dismissal, a narrowing and closing, if done in isolation from reckoning with the social relations of colonialism. Their analysis tells us something very important about teacher professional judgement, and with this teacher expertise more broadly. What knowledge is valued and whose voice is heard in policies about teacher professionalism and expert judgement is shaped across all levels of teaching practice and training. Addressing the social conditions of teacher expertise, therefore, is not just an academic exercise: it has real implications for what happens in practice – in policies, classrooms, staffrooms and wherever teachers' expertise is shaped and expressed.

Reflecting on contemporary social debates surrounding expertise, truth and evidence, we take 'teacher expertise' and problematize it as a product and expression of the value-laden conditions that assign and authorize it in the realm of teacher education, policy and practice. In doing so, we want to highlight that certain ways of knowing have been historically privileged, which has shaped who can speak as an expert, and to what ends. A foundational premise of our argument is that expertise is not a concrete, apolitical construct that is easily definable (or defensible). Nor is it something that can be rendered 'rigorous' or more 'politically neutral' through the 'correct' application of data, evidence or standardization.

Thus, the key questions for teacher education are those that surround who is – or is understood to be – an expert, what forms of knowledge is their expertise based upon and what practices does this expertise produce? There is a long and contentious history over who occupies the authority over teachers and their practice. The broad research field on teachers and teaching has examined the relationship between teachers and their autonomy, professionalism and expert status (see Chapters 4 and 5 for discussion of this literature). Often in these works, the problem for professional expertise is defined as the space between teachers and whatever new (usually external) authority is steering their practice. We have done this in our own work. For instance, Gerrard (Gerrard & Farrell, 2014) has written about how the Australian Curriculum was a powerful standard-based policy intervention into the expert authority of teachers, while Holloway (Brass & Holloway, 2021) has written about the hierarchical control of teachers' work through standards, targets and metrics. Our conclusions in these papers are like many of our colleagues' – that the expert authority of teachers matters immensely, and that trust in teacher judgement and expertise must be at the centre of understanding the possibilities for teachers and their work. As we will continue to argue throughout subsequent chapters, we maintain a similar position to these conclusions. Specifically, we see the outsourcing of expertise to data scientists, Big Tech and other non-education corporate actors as thoroughly incompatible with securing schools as equitable, democratic or socially just.

However, even when centring and defending teacher expertise, there is also a need to address the fact that experts and expertise cannot be pulled out of external interference to be pristine, neutral and good. In other words, while trust in teachers may be necessary and desirable, so too is a critical scepticism towards calls for a blanket trust in expertise (even when it's teachers). We view these positions not as contradictions, but as necessarily existing in tension. Thus we ask readers to move into an in-between space, where 'expertise' isn't easily definable, and the 'teacher' isn't a neutral good subject. Rather, we ask that teachers (and their expertise) are understood as being shaped by the conditions of a certain time and place. Following the lead from the work of Indigenous Gamilaroi scholar Bishop and colleagues Vass and Thompson (2021), Indigenous Pueblo scholar Calderon (2014) and Indigenous Gomeroi/Gamilaraay scholar Moodie and colleague Patrick (2017), who all call for decolonizing knowledge and practices within schools, we aim to problematize teacher expertise as part of broader societal assumptions about who and what counts as 'expert'. We move now, therefore, to a reflection on the position of expertise in society more broadly, before considering teachers and teaching more specifically.

Enough of Experts?

In 2017, UK MP and former Justice Secretary and Education Secretary Michael Gove decried, 'People in this country have had enough of experts!'. Later, responding to the ensuing public dismay and confusion over his statement, Gove clarified to the BBC's (2017) *Newsnight* that he was referring to 'organisations like the IMF' and their interpretation of the UK Brexit referendum, stating that it was important not to shy away from challenging experts just because they work for such organizations or are 'tenured academics'. Gove's comments capture a broader discontent surrounding the legitimacy and authority of experts emblematic of the so-called post-truth era. From the climate crisis and vaccine hesitancy in the midst of the Covid-19 global pandemic, the role of expertise has come under considerable public scrutiny (see Mede & Schäfer, 2020; Newman & Clarke, 2018). It is fair to say the institutions that are presumed to hold the authority to produce – or at least verify – facts and 'truth' (e.g. government officials and agencies, universities, media, schools), have become sites of contentious knowledge claims and even deep mistrust (see Bergmann, 2018; Block, 2019).

From anti-maskers and anti-vaxxers to climate change deniers and US Capitol insurrectionists, the chasm between those who deny the authority of experts and those who don't seems to be growing exponentially. To be sure, Gove's sentiments evoked a long-standing tension between 'the people' and 'experts', paradoxically spouted by someone who is a political expert of sorts, and who has benefited from one of the most prestigious and elite expert institutions – the University of Oxford (having completed his undergraduate degree there). Nevertheless, his remarks signal the contemporary emergence of the proclaimed post-truth zeitgeist characterized by a fundamental challenge to the function of experts and the authority of traditional expertise (see also Rosenblum & Muirhead, 2020).

In response, it is not uncommon to hear the proclamation to just 'shut up and listen to the experts'. As academics, we hear it among our peers. It has been plastered across major news media, and there are endless memes on social media portraying sceptics of the experts as ignorant or deserving of harm. In a lot of ways, this all makes sense. It is perhaps easy to dismiss many of the contemporary challenges as baseless populism and to double down on the need and respect for expertise. Certainly, the declaration of the 'post-truth' era appears to give strength to the argument for more expertise, as opposed to – for instance – opinion and hearsay. In the face of the unforeseen social, environmental, economic and medical crises of Covid-19, and those of climate change, to take just two examples, it is quite reasonable to appeal to a trust in those who have spent their lives developing the relevant expertise. Scientists face a hostile political environment in which scientific evidence of climate change is routinely ignored or dismissed. Countering this, 'Marches for Science' held in cities across the globe in April 2017 argued for a respect for the knowledge traditions of science and for 'evidence-based policy' (see www.marchforscience.com; see also Lubchenco, 2017). This response appears particularly sensible when the stakes are high and specialized expertise is vital for guidance through these deadly, uncharted waters. Certainly, expertise – and the rigorous production of knowledge via transparent and ethical research practices – does matter. Covid-19 demonstrates that the current moment is not defined by a withering of expertise, but its reconfiguration in relation to what is known and unknown (and asserted to be known and unknown), and by whom.

However, expertise is neither neutral nor categorical. Experts do not float disinterestedly above social relations. They are made by society and they have vested interests in making particular versions of society (see Rose, 1993). This is challenging terrain for those of us who are experts in some way, as researchers, teacher educators or teachers. Yet, facing the relationship between society and expertise is not an attempt to delete expertise, but rather to address the inevitable power relations of expertise that has meant that experts and expertise can at times be 'dangerous'. In other words, experts sometimes *do* violence, *do* further marginalize, *do* exacerbate inequalities. So, without putting aside critical questions about how societies will navigate the challenges they will inevitably face through drawing on expertise, we see an equally important need to challenge the taken-for-granted social assumptions that are often associated with experts and expertise. Indeed, in many ways, the debates between trust versus denial of expertise obfuscate the underpinning ever-present problematic of expertise: that it is a historical, political and social construct, even if and when verified by professional codes, knowledge and cultures.

To advance an argument that problematizes expertise in this way could be considered unwise. After all, we ourselves are experts, and we are writing to an audience of experts – teachers, students, researchers, teacher educators and policy makers. To push our reflections in Chapter 1 further, isn't writing a book that problematizes expertise written by experts to experts the undoing of ourselves? It is important to note then, that to problematize expertise and to situate it historically, socially and politically is *not* to deny its existence or utility. Rather, it is to do the essential work of understanding the power dynamics that underpin expertise that shape who is understood to be an expert in education and what kind of knowledge is valued. In the current context, defined on the one hand by a populist challenge to expertise, and on the other hand by a framing of expertise as something that can be neutralized through sophisticated data techniques and evidence, there can be a tendency to want to defend teacher expertise; to assert its importance within teacher professionalism against anti-expertise or overly datafied approaches. However, we suggest that rather than blindly defend expertise, what is urgently needed is an examination, and developed understanding, of expertise *as* situated, political, social and ultimately interconnected with the power relations of the day.

Teachers, 'New Empiricism' and Post-Truth

The need for grappling with the contradictions and complexities of expertise is particularly important when it comes to teachers. While their professional standing may be constantly under debate, their social role as experts shaping the future and interpreting the past and present cannot be understated. Teachers are one of the most significant groups of experts, charged with educating the next generation and working in institutions (schools) that have heavy investment and interest across society, including governments, parents, students, and – increasingly – corporations and large international agencies. The field of education is faced with multiple and competing agendas surrounding the constitution of expertise, trust in expertise and exactly what counts as expertise. There is no shortage of debate surrounding the authority of professional judgement in the context of evidence, data and standards (Garver, 2020; Hardy, 2019; Mockler & Stacey, 2021). While we explore the question of data in greater depth in Chapter 5, here we reflect on the contemporary uses of evidence as a means to address how teacher expertise is socially constructed and embedded, framed in the contemporary moment by vexed deliberations surrounding professional authority.

It is fair to say that internationally, the field of education has become focused on the question of measurement in part enabled by new technologies of data production and global imperatives surrounding standards and competition (Grek, 2009; Rizvi & Lingard, 2009; Sellar & Lingard, 2014). For many, the solution to debates on teacher expertise and professional judgement lies in more alignment to new forms of data, evidence and performance measurement. Take for example these two quotes from renowned international education expert Pasi Sahlberg and the US-based What Works Clearinghouse (WWC):

If we have learnt anything in 2020, it is that we need to learn to act in education more like we act in medicine. We should stop claiming that there is an extensive evidence base behind suggested educational treatments like the School Success Model without being sure about their possible side effects to children's learning.

(Sahlberg, 2021)

For more than a decade, the WWC has been a central and trusted source of scientific evidence on education programs, products, practices, and policies. We review the research, determine which studies meet rigorous standards, and summarize the findings. We focus on high-quality research to answer the question 'what works in education?'.

(WWC, n.d.)

While Sahlberg and the WWC approach the question of evidence from different standpoints, with Sahlberg suggesting greater account of the limits of the evidentiary basis for reforms, both ultimately frame the question of 'what works' as a question of data, evidence and the rigour of science. Sahlberg even draws on what has become a familiar refrain in the field of education, that we should be more like medicine (McKnight & Morgan, 2019).

At first glance, the rise of data and evidence to enact teacher professionalism and the challenge to expertise wrought by post-truth may only appear loosely connected, coincidentally occurring at the same time. However, these two seemingly divergent debates and positions circle around the authority of expertise and the truth and trustworthiness of expert knowledge and judgement. It is impossible, therefore, to treat these phenomena as distinct from each other (see also Wescott, 2022). This is what sociologists Anne Kelly and Linsey McGoey (2018) mean when they suggest that one way to transcend the seeming impasse between 'post truth' and intensified faith in certain kinds of scientific data ('new empiricism') is to recognize that both are intensely invested in what 'truth' is (see also Mede & Schäfer, 2020).

In their discussion, Kelly and McGoey (2018) highlight that any understanding of truth and expertise needs to consider the ways in which evidence, and the refusal of it, is linked to political power. Take the example of random control trials (RCTs) – experimental research based on the scientific veracity of intervening on a trial group and comparing results against a control group that has received no intervention. RCTs have become the 'gold standard' in some quarters of social and educational research and practice (such as the WWC quoted above), deemed to be the most salient and reliable methodological forms for understanding educational practice. Reflecting on their rising significance, Kelly and McGoey (2018, p 16) point out that the 'ecstatic' 'faith' that surrounds the empirical data of RCTs belies the inevitably incomplete character of the data they produce and the reality of political decision-making. Not only do RCTs only generate particular kinds of understandings that often bracket out powerful other explanations for educational practice (e.g. social relationships, structures, contexts, cultures and environments), they are also not the policy and political elixir that they are often represented to be. Kelly and McGoey argue that decisions surrounding policy and practice often rest upon the *absence* of data and at other times rest upon *wilfully ignoring* data (ideas that we explore further in the next chapter). RCTs are not a silver bullet for solving the problems of education and schooling; nor are they (or any other form of scientific research) going to be reliably followed in policy decision-making, given the political character of policy (as many educational researchers have already noted in relation to the fantasy of 'evidence-based policy' – see e.g. Biesta, 2010; Krejsler, 2013; Lingard, 2013; Wiseman, 2010).

Kelly and McGoey's discussions are helpful in situating teacher expertise *in* society. In a field such as education which is social at its heart, their point demonstrates the perpetual incomplete nature of evidence, expertise *and* their complex relationships to policy and practice decisions. RCTs and other forms of reified scientific methodologies, such as meta-analyses (e.g. John Hattie's *Visible Learning,* 2008), can never 'capture' the diverse social relations, cultures, economics and politics that create, and are created, in any school or classroom (Gale, 2018; Morrison, 2001; Wrigley, 2018). Indeed, in the preface of Hattie's highly influential *Visible Learning*, he explicitly brackets so-called out-of-school factors (e.g. poverty, family resources) from his analysis, despite noting their likely greater influence on schooling achievement (2008, p viii). This effectively produces an arbitrary line between 'in' and 'out' of school, and thus limits the scope of its insight about teachers, their work, and their influence. The point is that these sorts of more quantifiable methodologies cannot escape being steeped in the messy realities of social life and nor can they escape their own limitations. Quantitative claims about teachers' work are not freed from the questions of bias that are often levelled at qualitative claims. Indeed, messy social realities *are* the conditions of any research, and of teacher expertise and expert judgement: it is not possible to extract unspoiled forms of expertise that are untainted or unconcerned with the broader social, political and cultural conditions of possibility, no matter what statistical or data measure is placed alongside it.

The Social Conditions of Teacher Expertise

It's useful to contextualize the contemporary yearning for scientific certainty in teacher expertise in relation to the past and present production of expertise and scientific claims about the human condition. As should be clear by this stage, in this book we are less interested in prescribing or describing codified practices internal to teacher expertise, and more interested in how to understand these practices as socially contextualized, as a social relation. This shifts attention from codifying expert practices to reflecting on, and addressing, how certain forms of teacher expertise, and how certain teaching experts, become legitimized and authorized in the field of school education.

For some, conceptualizing what it is to be a 'professional' who exercises expertise requires undertaking a fairly objective task of identifying characteristics that define the profession apart from non-professional occupations. Jackson (1970, p 10) describes this process as creating walls around professional groups. This static or trait approach employs the notion that professionals are 'infallible experts' (Elliot, 1991, p 311), members of largely homogenous groups having common identities, shared sets of values governed by norms and universal codes of behaviour (Ozga & Lawn, 1981, p 13). However, this approach perpetuates a narrow vision of a profession, ignoring not only diversity within the profession itself, but also interaction between members of the profession, other groups and society (Ozga & Lawn, 1981). This model presupposes that expertise and experts (and the society within which they are enacted) are static and stable rather than ever-changing, challenged by communities and experts themselves.

The meanings and practices of teachers as experts are made possible by particular societies and make possible particular societies; and these dynamics are central to the production and expression of expertise. Teacher expertise is a part of the social relations of governance wedged between governments, students, parents and corporations. Rose (1993, p 297) writes, expertise 'should not be seen naively as a flowering of unbiased and concerned humanism, nor cynically, as merely evidence of professional entrepreneurialism'. Experts invariably articulate, and are articulated by, contemporaneous practices of the 'good life' and what it is to be a 'good citizen' in complex ways (see also Newman & Clarke, 2018). Take, for instance, the eugenics movement – a movement that carried significant weight within the education field (see Jones, 2018). This was a movement, started in the late nineteenth century by Francis Galton (cousin of Charles Darwin), that advanced a (pseudo)science of the improvement of 'race'. At the heart of this 'science' was a judgement surrounding the superiority of some races (Anglo) and social groups. Programs of sterilization, for instance, were promoted for the poor and disabled, the colonized, and for Indigenous communities, all in the name of the so-called science of eugenics and in the name of 'civilisation' (see e.g. Brogberg & Roll-Hansen, 2005; Pegoraro, 2015). While contested at the time, eugenics was a form of expert judgement that had force. It demonstrates the deep links between colonial presumptions of inferiority and the construction of expert knowledge.

Of course, the so-called science of eugenics has long been proven to be untrue, a conflation of colonial moral claims to 'civilisation' steeped in racism, ableism, classism and sexism. Yet, the influence of determinant understandings of capability and intelligence remain. Indeed, many point to the continued influence of colonial notions of populations 'out of control' that retain intensive and invasive violences, such as forced sterilization (e.g. Oliveira, 2021). In education, powerful ideas of 'progress', 'development' and 'innate capacity' that spurred on the concerns of eugenics have become rearticulated in both cultural and (more 'palatable') biological forms. For instance, Sriprakash, Sutoirs and Myer's (2019) examination of education in postcolonial 1950s and 1960s India, traces the re-inscription of ideas of progress, developmentalism, and difference into psychological and cultural theories of development, when biological theories of differences became untenable in the aftermath of the Holocaust.

Addressing the contemporary context, Au (2013) chronicles the rising significance of high-stakes testing in the United States, highlighting the connections between eugenics and the continuing influence of IQ testing (and the educative practices of testing and streaming that surround it). Pointing to the racist and classist underpinnings of IQ tests and their effects, Au notes how education 'experts' – academics, teachers, bureaucrats – threw their weight behind administering psychological testing as a means to stratify education (and society). Indeed, the significance of this history-into-the-present cannot be overstated: arguably the influence of IQ and/or presumptions of cultural lack and deficiency are so taken for granted and systemic they are often overlooked when it comes to the contemporary meanings and practices of streaming, intelligence, capacity, school-to-work transitions and everyday pedagogy and curricula.

These examples demonstrate the ways in which experts and their expertise function *within* particular socio-cultural contexts as well as seek to *construct* particular socio-cultural contexts. As much as post-truth and 'fake news' is a threat to contemporary society, so too is blind trust in expertise. Experts exercise their expertise with vested interests: they must make normative judgements about the best course of action in relation to possible preferred outcomes. None of this is to dismiss or minimize the practices, skills and knowledge of experts: it could be argued, for instance, that the exercise of expertise *is* a normative judgement in answer to the perennial question, 'what is to be done'? Yet, at the same time, this authorial professional position is not unproblematic, particularly given that any answer to that question is invariably shaped by power, politics and contemporaneous understandings of humanity.

What Is Expertise?

At this point, we want to end this chapter with outlining how we are understanding expertise for the purposes of this book. Though the first several pages have likely provided enough caveats, we still want to state clearly that defining expertise is in itself a politically and socially informed act. In many ways, the chapters that follow will grapple with the myriad tensions that have arisen in the efforts to define, study and operationalize expertise in our own (individual and collective) work. Nonetheless, we conclude by articulating a working framework for how expertise might be understood in terms of its relevance, governance and authority – broadly and as it relates to teacher education specifically:

- Expertise is political. It is socially, politically and historically constructed and is steeped in power (Beck, 2015; see also Foucault, 1980).

- Expertise is authorized through complex social processes (Straßheim, 2015), and 'the expert' and 'expert knowledge' are accepted and made possible by the conditions of a particular time and place (cf. Foucault, 1980; Rose, 1993).

- The 'expert' exerts – or attempts to exert – authority in an epistemic sense (i.e. through their specialized knowledge) and in a political sense (i.e. through their relevance and influence in the political realm) (Straßheim, 2015).

These three dynamics, for instance, are powerfully demonstrated in the quotes from teacher trainees Curtis and Leanne at the beginning of this chapter (Marom, 2019), which show how expertise is political, authorized through social practices and steeped in judgements about its knowledge base and recipients, as well as its relevance in the political realm. As such, what forms of knowledge and being are understood as expert and as a part of expert judgement are not simply the product of research on 'what works' in classrooms: it is also about power and social relations. It is about who is included as 'knowers' and who it is presumed needs to be taught. Indeed, we would contend that much of the 'what works' agenda provides a smokescreen for pressing issues facing the schools and teachers at the moment – diverting from intensifying political debates about 'what counts' and 'who counts' (and who and what is excluded) in schools.

When setting the quotes of Leanne and Curtis in the context of recent debates surrounding the teaching of racism and 'critical race theory' in schools, for example, it is clear that teacher expertise is at the centre of intensifying moral and political debates of power, inequality and injustice. Challenging the place of critical race theory – a framework for understanding systemic and structural racism in social institutions and practices – in the UK parliament, for instance, the Equalities Minister Kemi Badenoch warned,

> We do not want teachers teaching their white pupils about white privilege and inherited racial guilt. Any school which teaches these elements of critical race theory, or which promotes partisan political views such as defunding the police without offering a balanced treatment of opposing views, is breaking the law.[1]

At the same time that Leanne and Curtis are struggling to find their place in teaching, contestations about the role of schools in addressing race, colonialism, gender, sexuality, class, power, inequality and injustice in schools abound. And yet, all of these social dynamics are already right there in the corridors, playgrounds, pages of the text books, pedagogical relations, in teacher training and education, and in the relationships of governance between schools, teachers and the bodies and governments that regulate and surveil them. It is these relationships that we turn to now.

CHAPTER THREE

Challenging Expertise, Ignorance and the Un/known

As lecturers who often teach prospective teachers and existing teachers, we are familiar with the weighted authority that having been (or being) a teacher brings to the field of education. Often when introducing ourselves to our students, we can feel the collective sigh of relief ripple through the room when we say – in addition to our doctorates and research experience – that we also have been teachers. Being a teacher is a powerful marker of expert authority in the schooling field: teacher expertise is often asserted via experiential and embodied means; to have expertise in education is to *be (or to have been) a teacher*. Indeed, critiques of government bureaucracies and education policy makers, as well as influential corporate education initiatives, are often levelled on the grounds that their architects lack the experience of being a teacher. A large part of the assertion of teachers' expert authority comes from classroom experience.

While not denying the importance of relevant experience for teacher expertise, we wish to reframe these debates.[1] We suggest that the asserted need for teaching experience in order to be an expert in teaching rests upon a relational dynamic between 'experts' and 'non-experts'. To put it another way, teacher expertise is constructed as holding particular forms of authority because teachers have done something (teaching) that others have not. In this chapter we examine an often-overlooked aspect of teacher expertise: how expertise is constructed in relation to who is understood to be an expert and who is not, and in relation to the known and unknown of teacher expertise itself. First, we set out how teacher expertise is constructed through a (constantly shifting) relationship between the 'expert' and 'non-expert' in education. Here we highlight contestations and challenges to this relationship by both students and parents, demonstrating that teacher expertise should not be understood as an essential 'good'. Second, drawing on the emerging field of 'ignorance studies' (agnotology), this chapter explores how the known and unknown (and what is understood or thought to be known and unknown) is central to teacher expertise.

Teaching Experts and Their 'Subjects'

On 13 July 1977, a group of students and parents gathered to protest the actions of the Headteacher of Hornsey School for Girls (London, England) – Miss Curtis. Many members of the Black Parents' Movement and Black Students' Movement, the protestors chanted 'Curtis Out, Curtis Out' and waved placards that read 'Black Students Say Get Curtis off our Backs!' and 'Curtis Insults and Provokes and Persecutes Parents and Students' (Gerrard, 2014; Stapleton, 1977). In a leaflet produced for the protest titled 'We've Had Enough Miss Curtis!' the parents and students of this mostly Black school listed their concerns:

> Miss Curtis picks on the girls and gives them the treatment. She has been suspending girls in a very subtle and underhanded way, like taking them out of the class, and keeping them hanging about in the corridor outside her

office for days. Miss Curtis has had the girls locked in the cupboard, and kept in the dining and medical rooms for days and weeks with no school work. This is Miss Curtis's unofficial suspension and often parents do not know about it.[2]

In response, the Chairwoman of the Board of Governors defended Miss Curtis, referencing her professionalism; 'Nobody could deny that Miss Curtis and her staff are highly qualified, dedicated and extremely hard-working teachers' (Stapleton, 1977). The students and parents, conversely, were represented as the troublemakers. As put by a conservative Councillor of the local Council, 'I stepped in because I didn't want a way-out group to take up the running' (Stapleton, 1977).

This parent and student-led protest illustrates the contested, fragmented and mutable social contract of teaching expertise: the presumption that through the creation of teachers (via teacher training, qualification and experience) teachers know best, or perhaps at least know more, about the education and development of children and young people than parents (and the children and young people themselves). Here, in the case of the protests against Miss Curtis, the young people and parents were arguing that teacher expertise was not a defence that Headteacher Miss Curtis could use to justify her racist actions, and that they – as parents and students – needed to exert their own authority over the school. In holding these protests, these students and parents were contesting teacher authority and expertise and identifying its racism. Importantly, this event was part of a broader emergence in England of a radical Black politics, led in large part by African Caribbean migrants (Andrews, 2018; Gerrard, 2013; Warmington, 2014). These parents and students, responding to their experience of institutionalized racism, were attempting to combat inequality and unfairness and claim educational authority for themselves (Gerrard, 2014).

Indeed, the 1970s was a significant decade in the social relations of expertise. Internationally, the 1970s and 1980s was a time when parents, patients and welfare recipients (to name a few) began to challenge the ways teachers, doctors and bureaucrats exerted control over their lives in ways that did not resonate with their own experiences and values (e.g. Tenenbaum, 1977; see Eyal, 2019). Such challenges attempted to bring lived 'experiential knowledge' into conversation with institutionally accepted forms of expertise. This, Newman (1995) suggests, brought forth new expressions of expertise that are now expressed in relation to notions and practices of citizen/community participation, user consultation and models of 'co-design'. Of course, there is a constant and complex interplay between experts and the communities and people they serve, that is often contentious. More recently, and as we noted in our opening chapter, experts and expertise have come under significant challenge: questions surrounding the legitimacy of expert knowledge (e.g. climate change) and the efficacy and trustworthiness of official processes and expert judgements (e.g. Trump's contestation of the US election) are part of a broader rise of what many describe as post-truth and fake news.

Underpinning these shifts and contestations surrounding experts is an unwavering, fundamental dynamic at the heart of expertise: the relationship between expert and non-expert, which is always shaped by power. Experts hold power to influence policy and practices, power to make decisions that impact the lives of others, and in some cases direct power over the lives of others even when they themselves might be subject to institutional and political constraint. For instance, teachers have and hold power when it comes to the lives of students and their families at the same time that their expression of expertise and power as professionals is constrained and governed itself, as we discuss further in the chapters that follow. Teacher expertise is constructed and practiced *in relation to* students as well as their parents and communities. This power is neither neutral and unproblematic nor necessarily oppressive and unjust: rather the power that underpins expertise can be *both* of these things (see Newman & Clarke, 2018).

Indeed, a large part of how teacher expertise is constructed is dependent on institutional practices that are themselves subject to inevitable change and renewal. Teacher expertise is a highly regulated institutional practice. Schools, the certification of teaching degrees via higher education institutions, and the regulation of the teaching profession by the state all provide the institutional basis for the signification of expertise and with this, experts, and their actions. In addition, the diverse and intensified interests in teachers and their work – from the nation state, to politicians, private industry and the broader community – mean that the exercise of expertise is never a pure endeavour. Professional standards, standardized testing and curriculum, the big-business production of textbooks and data platforms, and professional learning itself, are all 'in the room' when teachers make professional decisions in relation to their students (see Lewis et al, 2019; Mockler, 2015; Thompson, 2019; Williamson, 2014). Thus, while we want to highlight the expert/non-expert relation as central to the production of teacher expertise, we do not treat these two positions as stable or unified.

As such, the assertion of teachers' expert authority in schools is deeply contested. The lines in which professional expert judgement over curriculum, pedagogy and school organization is constantly made and remade as states and markets reconfigure their relations to schooling and teachers. Yet, while significant educational literature focuses on how expertise is shaped by government forces and powerful private policy 'agents' and 'entrepreneurs' (e.g. Hogan, 2016), here we draw attention to how teacher experts and their expertise are constructed in relation to non-expertise and popular or 'ordinary' knowledge. This is at the heart of the protests against Miss Curtis, and it is, we suggest, at the heart of how teacher expertise functions.

The teaching profession has had to face multiple and varied crises in confidence in response to major contestations, such as Indigenous, anti-racist, anti-sexist, disability and working-class rights campaigns in education. These campaigns are often led by parents, young people and children; the 'non-experts' who sit outside of the professional 'expertise' of schooling, but who are also in many cases its primary subject of concern. These challenges to the practices of teacher expertise demonstrate the contested and dynamic relationality of expertise. As such, challenges to the expertise of teachers, of curriculum, of teaching and learning practices and of the organizations of school systems pattern the history of schooling and have contributed to shifts in the ways in which expertise has been understood.

For instance, there is a long historical tradition of popular education and with this, diverse popular claims to education including alternative modes of pedagogy and curricula (see Crowther et al, 1999; Mayo, 2020; Rockwell, 2011; Tiana Ferrer, 2011). Such claims to popular education are inextricably connected to challenges to the practice of expertise, and the ways schools and the teaching profession understand their purpose. To be sure, the exercise of teaching expertise in connection to eugenics, ableism, colonialism and sexism to name just a few, all demonstrate the violence of experts. Such forms of expertise have been challenged through a fundamental up-ending of the relation between the expert and the non-expert, fundamentally up-ending too the social relations and institutions that underlay the formation and exercise of expertise.

Importantly, however, this is not to say that popular challenges to expertise are unproblematic. As recent events have demonstrated, popular challenges and the claim to know *against* expertise emerge from a variety of different political standpoints. Politically progressive *and* conservative versions of 'parent power' have variously sought to challenge teachers' expertise (see e.g. Gerrard & Proctor, 2021). For instance, in Australia, conservative politician Mark Latham has recently introduced a bill to parliament called 'Parents' Rights' to forbid the teaching of gender fluidity under the guise of the rights of parents. Similarly in Texas, a proposed 'Parental Bill of Rights' is attempting to wrestle control of children's education from educators to parents in direct response to curriculum materials that represent and describe LGBTIQ relationships and communities, and which address systemic racism. The point, therefore, is not that non-experts offer a righteous corrective to expertise, but that teacher expertise is invariably constructed *in relation to* the challenges, experiences and knowledges of so-called non-experts.

Knowing and Ignorance in Education

Building on this understanding of expertise as constructed by the expert/non-expert relation, expertise is also defined by the epistemological relationship between what is known and unknown (or what is presumed to be known and unknown). Teacher education is fundamentally focused on knowing and knowledge: how to 'know' when and how learning has occurred dominates considerations of professional practice. The very act of teaching is framed by the pedagogical development and delivery of knowledge. Moreover, and as we chart in Chapter 5, teachers' work is increasingly governed by a concern to capture the truth of teaching and learning through data metrics. These are understood as the evidence of teachers' work, and as a consequence, is increasingly positioned as the worth and value of teachers' work. In what follows here, we suggest that the debates surrounding the knowledge of teaching are well served by an engagement with the unknown, including how presumptions of the unknown construct teacher expertise.

In so doing, we acknowledge that at the same time as the so-called rise of the post-truth moment, we are also witnessing the twin importance of 'new empiricism' (see Kelly & McGoey, 2018) as we discussed in Chapter 2. The fetishization of evidence and data in education (see Holloway, 2021; Lewis & Holloway, 2019) must be understood in relation to what is not known as well as what is *claimed* to be not known. As McGoey writes (2012, p 31),

What are less examined are the political and economic
battles that hinge on the constant policing of boundaries
between the known and unknown, on the effort to maintain
either a convenient fiction of one's expert knowledge of
possible outcomes or a convenient fiction of the exact
opposite resource: the pretence that no action is possible or
advisable given the inevitability of future unknowns.

Here McGoey draws attention to perhaps an inconvenient
truth that many education scholars have long highlighted:
education policies, practices and expert judgements are often
not produced on the basis of evidence, but on a purposeful
avoidance or ignorance of evidence or in the absence of
evidence (see e.g. Lingard, 2013). As with other expertise,
therefore, teacher expertise is dynamically formed in relation
to the construction and presence of 'ignorance'.

In education, ignorance is most often understood in its
pejorative sense: something that can be remedied with good
teaching and learning and the right forms of knowledge. In
thinking through what it means to consider the unknowns
of teacher expertise, it is worth noting the significant list
of synonyms, often uncomplimentary, for ignorance. In her
exploration of the study of ignorance (agnotology), Croissant
(2014) lists, among others, bewilderment, blindness, crudeness,
darkness, denseness, dumbness, illiteracy, incapability, innocence,
simplicity, stupidity, unawareness, uncouthness, unscholarliness
and vagueness. Yet, rather than see ignorance as something that
can be simply overcome through education, or as something
to be remedied and feared, with Gross (2007, p 749), we
understand ignorance as pointing 'to the borders and the limits
of knowing, including the intentional and the unintentionally
bracketing out of unknowns'.

With this working definition, here we outline four key
ways that ignorance and the limits of knowledge in teacher
expertise are necessary for understanding the kinds of truth
claims in teaching and teacher education. In doing so, we show
how attention to the unknown brings forth a different set of

considerations and questions about practice, which challenge depictions of teacher expertise as defined by data collection and analysis of the impact of teaching. This is what Malewski describes as a shift from 'truth content' to 'truth effects' (in Malewski & Jaramillo, 2011, p 12). Truth effect, Malewski writes, 'is concerned less with traditional issues of validity and more interested in the study of how assumed truths impact knowledge and assumptions about the world' (Malewski & Jaramillo, 2011, p 12). He continues (Malewski & Jaramillo, 2011, p 12),

> [T]he study of truth effects raises questions over what forces shape systems of thought, corresponding perceptions of social and educational possibilities, and outlooks on the world. A central focus of epistemologies of ignorance involves the study of truths that contained within them the possibility for errors, partial truths, and the ambiguities associated with truths that do not easily extend beyond context and place.

Perhaps most importantly studies of ignorance highlight the ways in which knowing and not-knowing is part of a constant dynamic, and that this dynamic is connected to the conditions of possibility for knowledge creation, social relations of power, institutional policies and prerogatives, and the construction of the taken-for-granted norms and cultures, inevitable in any society.

Thus, to end this chapter we bring insights from agnotology to think through some of the ways in which a focus on ignorance can deepen and extend our understanding of teacher expertise. As famously put by Whitehead (1929), 'not ignorance, but ignorance of ignorance is the death of knowledge'. Thus, we are not representing agnotology as a field as a whole, but rather engaging with key contributions that we see as central for understanding teacher expertise. Ultimately, our argument is that attention to ignorance is a useful corrective in a field of education that has become increasingly obsessed with pinning down, determining and knowing teaching as a complete technocratic practice, rather than a practice that is mired in ethical and political challenges and value judgements. Agnotology also invites educators and researchers to consider their own limit points. Leander and Wæver put it this way, 'Expertise is valuable, authoritative and ahead precisely – and perhaps paradoxically – because it is specific and therefore necessarily incomplete, closemindedly narrow, ill-informed and ultimately ignorant' (Leander & Wæver, 2019, p 11).

Students as Ignorant

The first way ignorance is fundamental to the construction and practice of teacher expertise lies in the impact of developmental notions of knowing and intelligence. As noted above, the idea that there is a natural pedagogic relationship of knower/unknower between teachers and their students has been central to the past and present practice of teaching. This relationship is perhaps most emphasized in pedagogic relations between children and adults. Here, perceptions of ignorance are supported by presumptions of developmental differences in knowledge, experience and intellectual capacity. Nonetheless, this relationship is also expressed in adult-adult pedagogic relations, such as in teacher education as well as in policy reform. Indeed, systems of education are ordered and formed around this presumption: large class size ratios, pre-established curriculum directives and standards, and pedagogic practices that understand 'participation' as a means to the predetermined learning objectives, all circle around teacher experts as knowing, and students as unknowing. This is perhaps best exemplified by 'chalk and talk' depictions of teaching, whereby teacher expertise is understood to lie in imparting knowledge, which students are then expected to receive and incorporate into their own understandings of the world.

One of the most well-known challenges to this conception is Brazilian educator Paulo Freire's *Pedagogy of the Oppressed*

(1970). Freire's revolutionary pedagogical intervention into educational thinking cannot be understated. He articulated a growing recognition that traditional forms of educational practice, in which teaching was understood as the delivery of knowledge to students (the 'banking method' of education), was based on problematic assumptions that students were deficit and lacked agency when it came to learning. More recently French philosopher *Jacque Ranciere* put forward the notion of the 'ignorant schoolmaster' to challenge taken-for-granted hierarchies between teachers and students, knower and not-knower (1991). Of course, such hierarchies are produced and enacted not just through individual teachers and their students but also through unequal social relations, in which particular *kinds of* students are understood to be more or less knowing (see Gerrard, 2019). In other words, the idea that children and young people are less knowledgeable than their teachers is not an unproblematic product of human development: such hierarchies presume either developmental (in)capacity and/or a lack of experience in ways that can easily slip into presumptions of deficit and which ignore the impact and existence of racial, gendered and classed social inequalities that are reflected and refracted in classrooms.

While there is a long lineage of diverse scholarship that seeks to disrupt – and upend – these presumptions (e.g. Allman, 2001; Ellsworth, 1989; Gore, 1993; hooks, 1994; McLaren, 1998), this tension remains at the heart of the perennial expert/non-expert relation. Indeed, even the notable move to bring students into school policy and practice – such as in student voice initiatives (e.g. Fielding, 2004; Groundwater-Smith & Mockler, 2016) – is often thwarted by institutional constraints (e.g. initiatives lacking real meaning and impact) *and* broader power dynamics in which young people (and particularly marginalized young people) are understood to be troublesome and deficit (see Bragg, 2007; Mayes, 2020). Here, such endeavours must reckon with the resilient idea that children and young people are unknowers.

Strategic Ignorance

The second form of ignorance at play in the field of education – strategic ignorance – refers to the broader politics of governance and politics in teacher education. At times referred to as wilful ignorance, strategic ignorance is the deliberate and often-time institutional practices that purposely adopt blinkered approaches (see McGoey, 2019). While McGoey (2019) suggests that strategic ignorance can be, and is, deployed by those in all kinds of institutional positions and political standpoints, in the education field one of the most important expressions of strategic ignorance is in and through the governance of education. A poignant example of this is 'policy-based evidence' (a play on the term 'evidence-based policies'), whereby politicians and policy makers borrow strategically and selectively from evidence, choosing some forms of evidence while ignoring others, or even going so far as to produce the right kind of evidence to suit politically driven reforms. For instance, Chung's (2016) analysis of the feverish enthusiasm surrounding the 'Finnish model' of school education following Finland's high PISA scores demonstrates the attempt of – in this case England – to adopt and translate Finnish policies and practices. Chung shows that this attempt, first, fundamentally ignored significant contextual differences between the countries, and second, took a 'pick and mix' approach, selectively taking aspects of the Finnish system that were politically salient and desirable.

To be sure, there are countless uses of expertise and evidence to support politically expedient reforms, which overlook major aspects of educational practice or other ways of understanding (and constructing) the educational 'problem' in the first place (see Bacchi, 2000). Uses of expertise and evidence in educational reform can obscure as much as it can highlight. For instance, Vickers' (2015) examination of quality teaching reforms in Australia demonstrates the ways in which these reforms, which focused so intensively on the impact of teaching, glossed over systemic and structural factors that frame the possibilities for this impact (such as residualization of disadvantaged student cohorts in the public schooling system).

Ignorance-as-Erasure

A third central way in which ignorance can be understood in teacher education is in the erasures that occur when particular forms of knowing and being are normalized and assumed. To give just one example, take for instance the curriculum erasures that were highlighted by recent decolonial campaigns, such as the UCL (University College London) *Why is my Curriculum White*. This campaign sought to highlight the ways in which Anglo- and Euro-centric traditions within higher education curriculum were normalized and taken for granted, to the point that the erasure of other knowledge traditions, histories and ways of being was taken for granted and not seen. In his influential essay on 'white ignorance', Charles Mills argues that the refusal to address the legacies of Black slavery and colonization in the US supports an 'airbrushed white narrative of discovery, settlement and building' such that the intergenerational and continuing structural practices of colonialism are blinkered out of sight (Mills, 2007, p 31). For Mills, white ignorance refers to the widespread and systemic practices of racism that produce a social reality in which racial domination and exploitation is normalized. He writes, 'So white normativity manifests itself in a white refusal to recognize the long history of structural discrimination that has left whites with the differential resources they have today, and all of its consequent advantages in negotiating opportunity structures' (2007, p 28).

These forms of erasure underpin the so-called culture wars in which debates surrounding the memorialization of colonialists become understood as attempts to rewrite history. Here, the erasure of violence of colonialism and racism has become so entrenched that any attempt to remedy this erasure is interpreted as navel-gazing relativism. Ignorance in this sense is a collective and cultural form of denial, or perhaps of turning away from acknowledgement even when the social realities of inequality are in plain sight. It is both explicit (in direct forms of politics, policies and the practices of institutions) and tacit (in the everyday presumptions surrounding the deserving and underserving). Thus, in this case ignorance-as-erasure is about curricular decisions surrounding how to teach slavery, colonization and racism and the taken-for-granted value of Anglo history and culture above other histories and cultures (see Sriprakash et al, 2022). Yet, it is also the social relations between teachers and students that are crafted in presumptions about the value of students' cultural background, the cause and blame of their disadvantage, and the need for students to change to 'fit into' society.

Importantly, ignorance-as-erasure is strongly tied to strategic ignorance, in that it often relies upon governments or schools or experts strategically acting (or not acting). It exists, therefore, not only in the absence of action but also at times when action is taken. For instance, Indigenous Kamilaroi scholar Hogarth's (2019) reflections on teaching in rural Australia reveal the interwoven relationship between the 'cultural taxation' of Indigenous teachers who are asked to do so much above and beyond their teaching work *as* Indigenous members of staff, and the seeming inability to address inherent and latent racism in schooling practices. Moreover, arguably, intensifying reforms around professional standards are embedding systemic ignorance in the exercise of teacher expertise. This is seen clearly in Indigenous Gomeroi/ Gamilaraay scholar Moodie and colleague Patrick's (2017) analysis of teacher trainees' understandings of the Australian teacher standards that directly address Indigenous contexts and knowledge. In their research they highlight how the professional responsibility to address settler colonialism and Indigenous perspectives is understood as a difficult addendum to teacher professional standards. Here, even in the *presence* of standards that address Indigenous experiences, this presence erases a genuine reckoning with Indigenous perspectives as it occurs in a context within which the political, cultural, social and economic reckoning with settler colonialism is lacking, thereby fostering a continued ignorance.

Uncertainty and Scepticism

The final form of ignorance that we see as being pertinent for teaching is the realm of uncertainty and scepticism. As we explore in the following chapters, the governance practices surrounding teacher education have cultivated understandings and practices of teacher's expert judgement that are heavily framed by a reliance on observable data on student performance and teacher impact. While these practices are often framed as producing more reliable and better knowledge, they can never eradicate the unknown in teaching but simply produce different forms of unknowns and ignorance. For instance, while such data can describe some aspects of teaching and learning, there is a whole raft of systemic, structural, cultural, personal, relational and cognitive aspects of practice that are simply not represented but which are arguably more influential than teaching practices such as teacher feedback and clear lesson objectives. Class, experiences of racism, sexism, transphobia and homophobia, levels of school resourcing, forms of school leadership and community resources are all central to understanding teaching and learning but cannot be represented in classroom-produced data, or in large aggregated statistical measures that do not examine differential and qualitative experiences.

Indeed, perhaps the presence of the unknown is why the embodied and complex dynamics of teachers, and their expert judgements, are so often highlighted in the literature. It is not uncommon to hear people speak of the 'messiness of teaching' as a means to try and describe the ways in which teachers develop relationships and make decisions in real time in the classroom (e.g. Loughran, 2011); classrooms that are characterized by the particularities of who is in the classroom, and what they bring with them when they enter the room. Certainly, a growing field of 'affective' studies of education are attempting to grapple with what might be considered the emotional politics of education; the ways in which teachers (with students) create particular feelings, cultures and even 'vibes' through their actions (e.g. Oplatka, 2009; Zembylas, 2005).

Understood in relation to the concept of ignorance, these kinds of more-than-observable aspects of teaching are part of the invariable uncertainties of teacher expertise. Often it is in these uncertainties that key ethical and political questions emerge about the practice of teacher expertise; important questions about the values of the teaching profession and its role in society. We suggest, therefore, that these forms of uncertainties can be fruitfully coupled with the deep need for scepticism in expertise. Scepticism is a form of criticality; a means to acknowledge the limits of one's own judgement and knowledge, and to reckon with the realm of the unknown. Uncertainty is not always something that can be overcome, but rather is in constant relation to what is considered 'known'. We suggest, therefore, scepticism is a useful and necessary tool *of* the so-called science of teaching and teacher expertise. It is this scepticism that we take into the next chapter, where we explore the rising significance of teachers – and in particular 'good teachers' – in education policy internationally, and the ways in which this import has produced new forms of governance for teachers and teacher education.

CHAPTER FOUR

Governance and Teacher Expertise

Almost fifteen years ago, Raewyn Connell identified the ubiquitous concern for the good teacher in educational reform. She reflected,

> What is meant by a 'good teacher' has thus become a significant practical question. It is also important conceptually, since ideas about good teaching are embedded in the design of educational institutions, and lurk in our talk about curricula, educational technology and school reform.
>
> (Connell, 2009, p 214)

While Connell frames her contribution in relation to the rise of contemporary neoliberal policy, this tension between professional autonomy, governmental control and understandings of what makes a teacher a good professional has long characterized the field of education. Nearly fifty years before Connell's reflections on the good teacher, educational researcher Alexander Frazier similarly asked, '[H]ow do we define a really professional teacher?' (Frazier, 1963, p 97). Frazier lamented that teachers had been viewed as inept, poorly trained and were subject to constant scrutiny and control. He condemned the extreme measures that had been used to control teachers' work, from standardized curricula to rigid schedules, ultimately calling for greater teacher professionalism and autonomy. Such calls are echoed in the contemporary context, with particular contestation around how expertise and professionalism get defined and who gets a say in doing so.

Today, it is fair to say that internationally, policies have become intensely focused on the creation of good teachers, often expressed in terms of 'quality'. Quality has become a proxy in public debate for addressing the exercise of expertise, emerging as a powerful signifier for the worth, possibility, and effectiveness of schools and their teachers. Indeed, the fixation on quality teaching produces, and is an outcome of, a forceful 'cultural myth' surrounding schooling: 'that *the* key to educational success lies with the teacher', often to the detriment of attention to the political, social, cultural and economic bases of schools (Larsen, 2010, p 218 [our emphasis]; see also Berliner & Glass, 2014). To reference Hattie's (2008) *Visible Learning* again, even when it is acknowledged that the influence of the teacher pales in comparison to that of outside factors on student performance outcomes, it is teacher quality that continues to attract significant attention and scrutiny in policy and research (Larsen, 2010). Policy agendas and debates around quality teaching are ultimately about the governance of teacher expertise: they are about how teachers exercise their expertise, who gets a say about what constitutes their expertise, and how such expertise is developed and measured. At the heart of these questions of governance is the long-standing, yet always shifting, debate about where teachers' professional judgement starts and ends in relation to government and other regulative controls. Policy agendas to standardize curriculum and teaching criteria are as much about the status of – and control over – the professional role of teachers as they are about creating a common basis of knowledge in schools. Advocacy for curriculum standardization, for example, is often accompanied by outcries about the quality of teachers and/or the indoctrinating intent of teachers.

This latter issue has become particularly pronounced in the United States recently, where issues like the teaching of Critical Race Theory have become a flashpoint of political debate. While it is true that teaching is always a matter of politics and political tension, the current moment has made visible what is often mistaken for a neutral site of knowledge sharing. Or at the very least, a site that some believe *should* be neutralized through enforced standards and standardization. However, we follow other critical scholars who see schools as well as knowledge production and sharing as always being sites of contestation over societal values (e.g. Apple, 1996; hooks, 1994; Leonardo, 2009). From this view, expertise, as well as the experts who are authorized to produce and share their knowledge within and through schools (e.g. in creating standards, writing curriculum, etc.), sit squarely within the political domain.

Indeed, to say that there is political interest in teachers and teaching is to put it mildly: schooling and teachers are, in fact, key 'battlegrounds' whereby moral anxieties regarding the character and directions of society, and culture are waged in and through defining the scope and limit of teacher expertise and practice. Importantly, such anxieties are globally articulated and are constituted within circulating discourses of a particular time and place. What teachers do with their expertise, as well as how their expertise is controlled, is always political.

As we will stress in the last chapter of the book, we resist the urge to shy away from the politicization of these matters, and we encourage all educators to do the same. Instead, we question how an embracing of the political can create new possibilities for teacher expertise to be imagined and operationalized. First, though, we use this chapter to look specifically at the relationship between expertise, authority and governance (particularly in relation to the state and non-state actors). We posit that new actors and discourses are shifting the modes through which teacher expertise is constituted, as well as who is involved in setting teacher policies, agendas and goals. With a look across teacher education and teacher professionalism, we map the ever evolving and emerging roles of state, non-state and trans-national organizations in these spaces. This includes, for example, the shifting authority of the teaching profession in relation to external organizations (from large corporate publishers like Pearson, to intergovernmental organizations like the OECD) that increasingly influence educational practice and ideas, from standards and certification to teacher education and professional development. We attempt to show that what was historically thought to be the responsibility of the profession (e.g. licensure, standards, certification, etc.) is now primarily articulated through external bodies that play active roles in writing policy, setting standards, providing curriculum materials and establishing accreditation criteria for institutions of teacher education. In doing so, we pose questions about the contemporary role of teachers and teacher educators who, in many ways, are positioned as channels through which materials developed by external organizations are transmitted.

In what follows, we reflect on the governance of teacher expertise by focusing on two separate, but interrelated, sites: teacher education and the teaching profession. Both teacher education and the teaching profession are implicated in the struggle over expert authority – as a means for external authorities to impose their values and interests, but also as a site where certain types of expertise are produced, shared and certified. Yet rather than (only) fixing our criticism on powerful actors who have had an outsized influence on teacher-related matters, we also wonder how teacher-based actors and institutions, like teacher educators, teacher education (as an institution) and the profession, might also be problematized in relation to expert/ise production and control. To this end, we ask: How does teacher education and the teaching profession govern expertise, but also how is it governed *by* experts and expertise? We begin with teacher education.

Teacher Education

At the time of writing this book, the Department of Education in England is proposing an overhaul in the way that teacher education programmes are accredited by the government. The proposal seeks to subject all providers of pre-service teacher education to an intensified reaccreditation process to demonstrate that their programmes follow even more rigidly stipulated standards and criteria than they already do. For many teacher educators, this is an unnecessary and problematic step too far, that signals unwarranted government interference into – and standardization of – professional authority and autonomy of teacher educators in determining the already government-regulated teacher preparation programmes. This is how Professor Susan Robertson, then Head of the Faculty of Education at the University Cambridge put it (2021),

> If these reforms were implemented, we would find that delivering high-quality [education] would be deeply compromised, and we would have no recourse other than to not offer the initial training postgraduate certificate in education. ... We have an outstanding PGCE programme, for primary and secondary teachers, and what we are looking at with this highly prescribed curriculum and model of mentoring doesn't at all look like what we do. We would have to exit.

Her comments echoed many in teacher education who see the proposed changes as a 'wrecking ball' that may leave no other choice than to close many university-based teacher education programmes. Critics warn these closures will leave the field dominated by private providers of teacher education (e.g. Now Teach, Ark). The University College London's Institute of Education (2021) put it this way:

We understand [initial/pre-service teacher education] as an intellectual and ambitious professional endeavour that reaches beyond a skills-based or technical approach to teaching, as reflected in the Universities' Council for the Education of Teachers' statement about the intellectual basis for teacher education. By contrast, the [government's] Review presents teaching as general, easily replicated sequences of activities, based on a limited and set evidence base. This is undermining of teaching as an expert profession. The proposals also misunderstand and misrepresent the process of professional learning, as standardised and linear rather than unique to each student teacher. We are disappointed that the Review essentially positions (student) teachers as passive consumers of a narrow set of research findings as well as atomised chunks of knowledge.

These proposed changes, and the debates that surround them, provide a compelling case for thinking about how teacher expertise is governed through teacher education and accreditation processes, as well as who maintains the authority to make such decisions. The shifting requirements highlight complex struggles over who is involved in setting agendas within teacher education, and how those agendas are translated and enacted in policy and practice. Within this arrangement, how is teacher expertise determined, and what role do teacher educators (and teachers) have in such decisions? If teacher education is the means by which pre-service teachers obtain expertise through coursework, in-situ practicums and the like, then who controls (or should control) what these teachers should know? According to many leading teacher educators in England, such authority should centre the expertise that resides within university-based teacher education. At the same time, similar considerations should be made about how teacher expertise is officially certified through channels like teacher licensure, promotion and tenure. In various ways, teacher expertise is governed through a network of professional and bureaucratic means that are always in tension regarding what should be known and who gets to decide. Teacher education sits at the intersection of this complex assemblage.

On one hand, teacher educators maintain significant authority in governing teacher expertise, requiring continual reflection on how their construction and authorization of teacher expertise is responsive to the needs of society. At the same time, however, teacher education is also governed through bureaucratic and (increasingly) hierarchical means (cf. Evetts, 2013), such as through increasingly heavy-handed state-based accreditation systems that dictate how teacher education programmes must operate (see also Brass & Holloway, 2021). In this way, actors outside of the profession have access to the control and production of teacher expertise, ultimately determining what gets prioritized and authorized within teacher education institutions.

Another recent example where such tensions are made visible is in the United States, where accreditation has undergone similar changes to those in England. Prior to 2014, the United States had three major accrediting bodies that oversaw the thousands of teacher education programmes across the country. These accrediting bodies had direct ties to professional teaching organizations, as well as to university-based teacher education (Brass & Holloway, 2021). That was until the three bodies merged into one (i.e. the Council for the Accreditation of Educator Preparation, CAEP), requiring all teacher education programmes to answer to a single authority for determining their methods and content for training aspiring teachers (Brass & Holloway, 2021). These changes were happening at the same time as a new pre-service teacher assessment system was making its way through teacher education programmes across the country (i.e. the edTPA). Currently, the prescribed assessment system is used in '800 programs across 41 states and the District of Columbia' (SCALE, n.d., n.p.), and is also being adopted in other countries, like Australia (see Stacey et al, 2020). It is not (yet) a required component for accreditation in the United States, but it is marketed as helping teacher education programmes meet accreditation requirements (edTPA, n.d., n.p.). By contrast, in Australia all teacher education programmes are required to develop or adopt a similar form of assessment, significantly altering the power balance between university autonomy and state regulation (see Rowe & Skourdoumbis, 2019).

While debates about the content, reliability and validity of these accountability measures are important (see e.g. Berliner, 2018; Kuranishi & Oyler, 2017; Polly et al, 2020), in this book we are concerned with the implications regarding the tightening control over who gets to determine what counts as expertise, as well as the reduction in plural ways of approaching teacher development and assessment. This is particularly important when thinking about teacher education as a site for constructing teacher expertise and authorizing the teacher as an expert as universities and colleges of teacher education are subjected to increasingly tighter constraints over what they are required to include (and exclude) in their programmes.

In the context of the United States, the edTPA, for instance, requires teacher candidates to submit materials for assessment to the corporate publishing giant Pearson. In their participatory policy analysis of edTPA, Indigenous Unangax̂ scholar Tuck and colleague Gorlewski (2016) highlight how outsourcing these assessment practices to corporations means accepting context-free and apolitical measures of expertise. The result is, Tuck and Gorlewski argue, an entrenchment of racial inequalities whereby the situated, contextual and diverse realities of teaching are papered over in favour of standardized and so-called neutral accounts of good teaching. The issue at question here is that these standards treat teaching, and teacher expertise, as if it is disconnected from the deep inequalities and injustices that structure our world. Tuck and Gorlewski (2016, p 213) go on to reflect,

The edTPA as it has been adopted in New York State is exactly a case in which the problem has been defined so narrowly that the 'solutions' it will produce – teachers who have passed a standardized performance assessment without any occasion to reflect on the roles of race and racism in classrooms or schools – will change little to affect the everyday racist ordering of life in the United States.

Indeed, this policy is a good example of ignorance-as-erasure as explored in the previous chapter – an approach to teacher education and teacher expertise that glosses over, ignores, the very social relations that teachers are supposed to engage and respond.

Australia is another location where accreditation is undergoing significant changes, with one body governing teacher education – the Australian Institute for Teaching and School Leadership (AITSL). As part of the AITSL accreditation, teacher education programmes are also required to implement a teacher performance assessment (TPA) for teacher candidates (see Stacey et al, 2020 for a review). Like the edTPA in the United Sates, it is meant to assess whether teacher candidates can be certified as experts in their respective domains. Again, we are less concerned here with whether such assessments promote the 'right' version of 'good teaching'. Rather, we are concerned with the ways in which such forms of accreditation and regulation narrow, rather than widen, the field of experts authorizing what teachers should know and how that should be assessed. As Rowe and Skourdoumbus suggest (2019), these kinds of reforms are reducing the authority of teacher educators and educational researchers to influence and shape teacher expertise, let alone teachers themselves.

As we make this argument, however, we want to return to our point that teacher education also governs expertise, and therefore holds a responsibility for its politics, including its commitments to equality and justice (Ellis et al, 2019). We want to make very clear that historical versions of teacher education, and teaching practice, should not be romanticized. There are too many examples of how marginalized students have suffered at the hands of unchecked discretion to not take seriously the notion that accountability is necessary for achieving justice for students and their communities. For instance, addressing the issue of systemic racism, Picower (2009) argues, 'Teacher education must take seriously the negative impact that Whiteness can have on teachers' understanding of children of color and urban schools. White teachers are often entering the profession with a lifetime of hegemonic reinforcement to see students of color and their communities as dangerous and at fault for the educational challenges they face' (p 211). Therefore, as we caution against the retraction of agency and authority within teacher education programmes, we are not suggesting that there is a past or pure practice of teacher education to be rescued. Rather, we must also be frank about how all institutions, including those carrying out teacher education, are responsible for reckoning with the politics of knowledge and expertise and how these matters have often privileged the interests of some at the expense of others.

It's therefore important to connect these tensions over knowledge and expertise at the national to global levels as well. Concerns over how schools and teachers respond to current society, as well as their role in shaping future directions and priorities, are expressions of national agendas and projects of 'nation building' *in relation to* global prerogatives and historical contestations. Contemporary trans-national fixations on measures of excellence (e.g. PISA test scores) create, and are created by, processes of ordering, bordering and othering – defining oneself in relation to what one is not. This, of course, stems from ongoing trans-national relations of power, globalization, and associated effects of colonialism and white supremacy (the explicit and implicit, structural and personal, presumption of the superiority of 'whiteness', its institutions and cultures – see Cabrera, 2014; Gillborn, 2005; Mutekwe, 2015; Robertson, 2008; Sriprakash et al, 2022).

Thus, teacher education across national contexts is shaped by the converging global logics and discourses surrounding what 'good' education and 'good' teaching look like. The effects of this are felt both within these national contexts and outside. Expertise of the modern era has been governed and defined by the actors, discourses and knowledges of 'Western' thought (e.g. enlightenment-based thinking) and has been concentrated in the Global North. Consequently, much of the rest of the world, and especially post-colonial countries are often compelled to modify their image and practices to emulate the so-called best practices as determined by the Global North, often to the decimation of their Indigenous knowledge, language and values within schools (De Lissovoy, 2019; Mutekwe, 2015). This has been exacerbated by global orders of education reform, whereby schools and entire schooling systems are positioned in relation (and in competition) to one another (regardless of geographic location or socio-historic condition).

At the same time, global organizations like Teach for All (originating from the US-based Teach for America [TFA]) and the Organisation for Economic Co-operation and Development (OECD) continue to have significant influence over defining 'expertise' as it relates to teachers (Rizvi & Lingard 2009; Thomas et al, 2020). Trans-national organizations like TFA, the World Bank and the OECD, as well as educational capitalists like Apple, Google and Pearson, present important cases to consider because of their sheer reach. There are few education systems in the world that have not been influenced by both, and their authority over 'good teaching' is felt in schools and in teacher education (Biesta, 2019; Hogan et al, 2016; Lewis, 2022).

As we problematize teacher expertise as being shaped by various power relations and discourses, we must continue to cast our critical gaze in all directions – upwards at the hierarchical powers that have gradually restricted the space for teachers to exercise professional autonomy, but also historically and inwards where the politics of expertise also reside. On this note, we turn our focus to the teaching profession to explore how it is governed by, but also how it governs, teacher expertise.

The Teaching Profession

The understanding of teachers as 'professionals' and of teaching as a professional practice is not a given. This seemingly intractable question of the professional status and identity of teachers has significant implications for how teachers are also understood as experts. Sociologist Julia Evetts (2013, 2018) has written widely on the concepts of the 'profession' and 'professional'. She has argued that the idea of the professional has fundamentally changed over time, and that in more recent times, the governance of the professional has been increasingly subject to hierarchical, managerial and bureaucratic controls (2013, 2018). Both contributing to, but also a product of these discourses, is the reliance upon metrics, standards and evidence to shape teacher professionalism, development and accountability, not only through teacher education as discussed above, but also through the everyday practice of teaching. In the contemporary context, the setting of professional standards for practice and certification are not solely in the hands of teachers and teacher educators but are heavily influenced and defined by complex networks of external actors (Savage, 2020; Savage & Lewis, 2018).

The current debates surrounding teacher education and professionalism are connected to long-standing contestations surrounding the professional standing of teachers. That teachers are experts, with particular forms of expertise, is a presumption linked to – and enabled by – the notion that teachers *are* professionals. Yet teachers have always had a somewhat tenuous position as a profession. Questions of professionalism in teaching must be understood in relation to the historical and social significance of the 'feminization' of the profession. Historically, the feminization of teaching arose primarily from the mass expansion of schooling and the subsequent increase in demand for teachers. Schooling systems looking to increase teacher numbers chose to employ women as they were paid considerably less in comparison to their male peers, and women seeking independence and social mobility entered into a teaching career in high numbers as early as the 1880s (Apple, 1987, p 61). These changes to teaching occurred within a socio-cultural framework which defined women's work within the bounds of reproductive and domestic duties. It is therefore not surprising that teaching became a substantive career opportunity for women (Apple, 1987, p 62). It is also not surprising that teaching, and other female-dominated occupations were labelled semi-professional as the traditional view of women's work as bounded by domestic nurturing roles pervaded dominant cultural understandings.

Now, the tussle over exactly what is the professional status and role of teachers is characterized by a busy field of interested actors. Unlike medicine and law (historically dominated by men, though this is changing in the contemporary context), teachers do not have independent and autonomous professional organizations that govern and codify their conduct; rather they are enmeshed in – and governed by – the state. For instance, in Australia the governing body for teachers and teaching standards – AITSL – is appointed by, and accountable to, the government – not the profession. By contrast, the peak body representing the interests of doctors – the Australian Medical Association – is run and led by members (doctors), working with the government rather than by it. Teaching standards, schooling curriculum and the surveillance of teacher conduct are produced by governments (increasingly so), and while teachers may well be consulted (along with corporations, employers and other educational 'stakeholders'), or a part of the process of deliberation, ultimately it is governments who determine 'what counts' in relation to the codification of teacher expertise (in many parts of the world).

As such, significant debate has surrounded teachers and their work: Is it professional? Is it semi- or quasi-professional? To many in the field of education these questions serve as the foundation upon which expertise is built. Concerns of de-professionalism, for instance, are expressed in relation to a reduction of the capacity for expert judgement to be exercised, such as through the emergence of standardized curriculum and the increasing international reliance on privately produced curriculum materials, such as textbooks and direct instruction materials (Biesta, 2015). Bonal and Rambla (2003, p 171), for instance, describe this as the emergence of a 'new' teacher; a teacher who 'must become a knowledge manager rather than a knowledge expert', a purveyor of student capabilities. Such a teacher, according to Bonal and Rambla, 'becomes also responsible not just for educating the future workers' abilities but for socializing workers as 'good citizens' (2003, p 171). In other words, 'good' teachers make 'good' citizens, which is a common refrain throughout global reform efforts that position schools and teachers as solutions to the 'wicked', or seemingly intractable, 'problems' (cf. Churchman, 1967; Rittel & Webber, 1973) that ail societies.

In doing so, the risk associated with teachers and their expert judgement becomes so high stakes that it becomes entirely rational to place controls on what and how they teach, however misguided we might believe that to be (see also Hardy, 2015; Holloway, 2019). The prevailing discourse that is so deeply entrenched within the broader neoliberal articulations of schooling has framed teachers as crucial for ensuring everything from economic stability to physical and social wellbeing, to even climate crisis intervention (e.g. see National Commission on Teaching & America's Future, 1997; OECD, 2005). If we think about the responsibilities being imposed on teachers, then we can also see how their judgement to 'get it right' is considered so crucial. Rightly or wrongly, the discursive terrain that shapes our understanding of schooling as a site for managing personal and national risk has created a situation where controlling how teachers exert their expertise is somewhat hard to dispute. Thus, when we speak of how teacher expertise is governed, it is important that we not only consider what teachers need to know, but also how that expertise gets (mis)appropriated for various purposes. In other words, the problematization of 'expertise' does not only require questions about what teachers should know, or the degree of autonomy needed to exercise their expertise, but also about what teachers are expected to accomplish with their expertise.

That is, as the bureaucratic control of teachers' work has increased, so too has the expectation that teachers would carry the burden of societies' problems. Never has this been clearer than during school closures caused by Covid-19. Overnight, teachers were seen as frontline workers whose role in caring for young people, beyond academic obligations, became undeniable as the stability of the economy rested on parents being able to juggle home school and work. Newspapers flashed headlines of appreciation, and parents around the globe expressed newfound admiration for the daily work of teachers (see UNICEF, 2020; Victoria, 2020). To be sure, the impact of Covid-19 has taken its toll on teachers: from school closures; to the exacerbation of educational and social inequality; juggling parenting and working themselves; moving to 'online' learning; and managing competing demands including the fear of 'learning loss' and students' and communities' material, social and emotional wellbeing (see e.g. Baker et al, 2021). The wellbeing of teachers themselves has taken a toll (Baker et al, 2021; Beames et al, 2021), and now staggering teacher shortages are leaving schools – and entire schooling systems – calling for help (e.g. Carver-Thomas et al, 2021). In the context of where we write, for example, staff employed in bureaucratic positions within departments of education are being redeployed back into schools in an attempt to manage the crisis in teaching numbers.

Despite such untenable conditions, however, governmental responses continue to focus on *ramping up* the stakes and standardized requirements for teachers worldwide, and many teachers are ready to leave the profession altogether (Flannery, 2020; Heffernan et al, 2022). In the UK, a recent poll found that a staggering 44 per cent of teachers are planning to leave by 2027, mainly due to unbearable workloads that have only been exacerbated by the pandemic (Bateman, 2022). The continual turmoil surrounding teachers, their work and their role points to how the perennial concern surrounding the 'professionalization' and 'deprofessionalization' of teachers is a matter fundamentally entrenched in their working conditions and rights.

Indeed, the unionization of teaching and union activity of teachers are pivotal to teachers' claim of being a 'professional' and their entitlement to autonomous expert judgement (see Bascia, 2009). Without a governing professional organization that is member-run, unions are key organizations through which teachers express and defend their roles as professional experts, often alongside broader claims on the state of schooling (see McGrath-Champ et al, 2019; Symeonidis & Stromquist, 2020). For example, the history of the South African Democratic Teachers' Union highlights the (at times contested) interplay between debates about teacher 'professionalism' and expertise, teachers' conditions, and the role of teachers and schools in social struggle and change (see Kumala & Skosana, 2014). In this context, these debates were obviously focused on apartheid education systems and their ongoing effects in racial oppression and inequalities. This example points to the broader politics of the claim to professional identity and the kinds of responsibilities that *being* a professional is thought to bring that goes beyond (or rejects and challenges) the implementation of standardized curriculum and achievement scores on large-scale standardized tests. Such considerations reverberate in and through a range of union contestations across national contexts, including for example the 2012 Chicago teachers strike (Uetricht, 2014; see also Charney et al, 2021)

Thus, what constitutes 'professional' and 'professional judgement and status' is neither stable or universal, and nor is it judged uniformly. For instance, prescribed professional standards are heralded by some as 'professionalising' teachers, and decried by others as being the hallmark of 'deprofessionalization' (White, 2010). Bascia (2009, p 481) aptly describes the tension in the claim to 'professionalization' this way:

> Even when teachers use the term [professional] positively, it can mean many different things: individualism or collectivity,

compliance with administrative regulations or autonomy, technical competence or political strength, protectionism or altruism. However ambiguous its meaning, professionalism is always a highly charged concept: merely posing the question of whether or not teachers are professionals introduces the possibility of doubt: perhaps they are not; perhaps, in other words, teachers' innate skills, training, and individual and collective behaviour are not worthy of respect.

For example, in the context of Australia, Chatelier and Rudolph (2018) explore the paradoxical nature of heralding 'professionalisation' in stipulated standards. In their examination of professional standards related to special needs teaching, they suggest such stipulated regulations and standards create performative agendas for teachers that move the profession away from deeper ethical and inter-subjective considerations of teacher-student relations.

In light of these arguments, perhaps it is a good time to question whether the de/professional debate is adequate or useful for capturing the dynamic nature of teaching. In many ways, the divide often obscures historical and contemporary differences within the field regarding what it means to be professional. A recent project one of us (Holloway) conducted with teachers in Australia, England and the United States found significant differences across teachers (even among teachers within the same schools) regarding how they see professionalism. One conversation comes to mind that demonstrates the complex – and at times contradictory – claims made about professionalism and deprofessionalism in the contemporary moment. When discussing the imposing structures of accountability and prescribed curriculum demands, one teacher – Tanya – viewed standardized expectations as making her *more* professional.

The following is an excerpt from the interview with Tanya. The context of the discussion is focused on new requirements about data use and reporting. The teacher had taught previously and had recently returned after a several years' break, and she reflected on the major differences she noticed upon her return:

> *Tanya:* [The major differences are] really about structure. Before I left, the nine years, it was very teacher influenced data; it was your own decisions; you know, 'teaching your best'; you could really assess however you liked, formative or summative. It was up to you, whether it was anecdotal notes or whether you actually had formal documentation; it wasn't really seen as an issue. It was just, the teacher was kind of - they were in charge of it; it was their decision. We didn't plan together then, as well, before I left. So I think planning and assessment are so closely linked. And a school like this, because we are so big – so the Year 4s have seven classes, 26. It is a mini-school, really. Before I left, we didn't do any planning together. We just knew the curriculum; did your thing; assessed however you liked; and spat out a report at the end of the year.
>
> *JH: Can you talk about the structures?*
>
> *Tanya:* We plan together, so everything is done together … . Once a week, two-hour block; we all plan together and then we discuss it before we separate; so everyone knows exactly what's happening across every subject area of the week. Then our testing, or any type of assessment we do, is all coordinated; and whether that's summative or formative or 'how are we looking at that'; and then when we get back together, we always have 15 minutes to half an hour looking at assessment across the team of seven each week. We actually draw all of our assessments together at the start of each session and it varies all the time, and then we plan from there.
>
> *JH: So what are your thoughts about that?*
>
> *Tanya:* Very structured. I really like it accountability-wise. It is full-on. I feel like teaching-wise you are all in or you are not in.

JH: You can't have an off-day, huh?

Tanya: No off-day, no. It's a lot of – yeah. I don't really feel it is pressure; because I kind of feel like it takes pressure off a little bit. Only because – well, it is not your judgment all the time. So the pressure on you to make the call all the time -

JH: That is interesting, yeah; the distribution of responsibility?

Tanya: Yeah, yeah, we are all – yeah. And because we moderate so much now –

JH: – to make sure that you are all judging the same way?

Tanya: Yeah, all the same way. But we also kind of do that with Maths as well because we talk about the Maths so much, as seven classes as a mini-school, really. Yeah, I feel like it takes the pressure off a little bit, which is weird because you think – it is more – it's kind of hard to explain. It is more pressure that you are on. I guess it just seems more professional. Maybe that's what it is. It is just, yeah, 'You are in this', and it's – I feel like it's more than a job now.

JH: What do you mean by that?

Tanya: You live it, breathe it; like, it's consuming.

In Tanya's account, standardization was connected to her experience of increased collaboration with her peers and a sense of working together, rather than in isolation. Of course, every school is different, and this particular account of collaboration will not mirror all contexts. However, what this excerpt demonstrates is how a professional/de-professional divide does little to capture the complex interplay of teacher experience and conditions that shape their understanding of their own expertise and their enactment of it.

A significant part of this is the changing teacher workforce, as a new generation of teachers, who have often experienced intensified standardized schooling as students, enter schools with no other way of knowing how to approach or judge their work in the classroom. In England, Wilkins (2011) called this new generation the post-performative teachers (cf. Ball, 2003), or those who felt differently than their more veteran colleagues about school policies that emphasize competition, evaluation and metrics. In his argument, even though the common sentiment was that greater bureaucratic controls were an imposition, the early career teachers he interviewed were more likely to dismiss such complaints. He (Wilkins, 2011, p 401) quotes one of his teacher participants as saying:

> I have to hold back sometimes when people moan about paperwork ... to be honest I think they are hanging on to the past where teachers could get away with murder. I couldn't do my job without the paperwork.

This emergence of a new settlement surrounding teachers and professionalism is further demonstrated in Good's (2021) research with teachers in the US Midwest about their understanding of expertise. Their definition was a resounding: 'it depends'. This sentiment only reinforces that teacher expertise is a complex interplay of factors that are highly dependent on context, purpose and perspective.

Indeed, it is important to note that contestations surrounding teacher professionalism are not just about the definition and exercise of 'professionalism'. Indigenous Lumbee scholar Brayboy and colleague Maughen's (2009) research with Indigenous teacher trainees in the United States, for instance, highlights the ways in which histories of educational exclusion and marginalization impacts how Indigenous teachers can and do claim their authority and professional identity within the profession. Here, Indigenous teacher trainees understood their professional ethics and duty in relation to their own personal and collective experiences of educational injustice and trauma (2009). Being 'a professional' is about an intervention into past and present professional practice. This demonstrates that the challenge for the teaching professions is not just further diversity and inclusion of the teaching profession, but a reckoning with the violence of an expertise that presumes its universality and its righteousness.

All that to say, there is some danger in trying to squeeze the state of teaching into the mould of either being a profession or not. To do so completely misses the nuances that reside within the field, and has the potential to mistake historical practices as being better than what currently exists, or vice versa. It is also worth noting that the contemporary urgency surrounding teachers, their work and their professional identity is not new (as demonstrated by both Connell's and Frazier's concerns quoted at the beginning of the chapter). It is perhaps understandable that contemporary claims surrounding 'professionalism' and 'de-professionalism' slip into an implicit judgement that professional capacities once existed, and are now being lost. Yet in actuality the processes of professionalism and de-professionalism are cyclical and ever-present. Back in 1999, Theobald put it this way (p 30):

> We discover anew in each generation that the mass profession is also the Cinderella profession; that teachers do not have the status they deserve; that the interest of men in teaching is in inverse proportion to the age of the children to be taught; that women carry the burden of classroom teaching; that our brightest and best of either sex will not enter the profession. We agree over and over again that in a democratic society where education is vital to life chances these things should not be so. It is understandable that in each generation we cast about us for explanations readily to hand. But we build on shaky foundations indeed if we do not acknowledge that there is no golden past to which we can return.

This is not to say that there are not clear policy agendas and practices in the current moment that can be seen to be impacting upon teachers' exercise of expert judgement and their professional status (e.g. increasing standardization, the rise of global and local metrics, the scope and scale of private actors in teaching and learning delivery). Indeed, we use the next chapter to look specifically at these issues and how discipline-specific expertise, like economics and data science, have sought to neutralize teacher expertise. However, we also wish to emphasize that questions surrounding teachers, their work and their judgements always have, and always will, exist.

CHAPTER FIVE

Data, Knowledge and Expertise

As we hope has been made abundantly clear thus far, we take the construction of expertise as something that is always in the making (and re-making). It is a product of discourses, of practices, of social and historical conditions, and it is never neutral. It is always historically, politically and socially contingent, and thus it is always up for critique. Even as we (as teachers, researchers and teacher educators) may claim and defend the expert status of teachers, we must apply the same critical eye upon our own subjectivities, privileges and environments that shape our understandings of teachers and teaching. In this chapter, we zoom in on two specific discourses that have profoundly influenced these understandings in the current moment – economics and data science.

What we focus on are the logics and tools of these disciplines and how they have defined expertise, including the type of expertise teachers are meant to use for understanding students and their performance, as well as the types of expertise used for assessing whether someone is a good teacher. This includes, for example, how teachers and teaching have been subjected to (and have become *subjects of*) logics of metrics, data and evidence, such as value added measurement for assessing student and teacher performance, as well as the ubiquity of

data dashboards and surveillance in schools. As we explore
below, these conditions have ushered in new technologies,
techniques and actors that have significant implications for
teacher expertise.

First, we look at the various forms of expertise that
have influenced education (broadly) and teachers/teaching
(specifically). We do this to reiterate that expertise is
constructed as a product of power relations, but also to show
how 'teacher expertise' cannot be understood as *separate from*
the various forms of expertise that underpin the technologies
and discourses of education broadly. Finally, we bring these
threads together to think about how a teacher's expert status
is brought into question, monitored and evaluated. We start
by taking an historical look at the 'datafication' turn in
education.

Datafication of Teachers and Teaching

It will be no surprise to readers that the past three or so
decades have seen an ever-increasing emphasis on testing and
evaluation as key, global features of teacher policy and practice
(Grek, 2009; Smith, 2016; Verger & Parcerisa, 2017). From
standardized testing schemes at the national and subnational
levels, to international large-scale assessments (e.g. PISA;
TIMSS and PIRLS), testing has become a key instrument to
measure, evaluate and compare various aspects of schooling.
This includes, but is not limited to, school performance,
national rankings and, in many cases, teacher performance and
quality (Smith, 2016; Verger et al, 2019). Often in the name of
equity and accountability, teachers have been subjected to a
number of test-based instruments that are used to quantify and
define their performance and comparative value (Ball, 2003;
Perryman & Calvert, 2020). Many have argued that in doing
so, teacher performance has been reduced to that which can
be measured (Garver, 2020; Mockler & Stacey, 2021), while
simultaneously shaping teaching practice accordingly.

Indeed, extensive, international evidence has shown that almost all teachers face some sort of appraisal that incorporates student test scores into the judgements of their performance (Smith & Kubacka, 2017). For example, in England, Ball (2003), Bradbury and Roberts-Holmes (2017), Perryman (2009), Pratt (2016), Pratt and Alderton (2019) and Wilkins (2011), among others, have found that such measures have changed not only the role and responsibilities of the teacher, but also who the teacher *is* and how their relationships with students are structured. Their argument, which has been similarly raised in other national contexts (e.g. in the Netherlands, see Browes & Altinyelken, 2021; Norway, see Camphuijsen et al, 2021; in Chile, see Avalos-Bevan, 2018), is that the hyper-focus on testing and metrics, in conjunction with systems of dis/incentivization, has produced teachers who must comply with expectations of competition, surveillance and test-based instruction. Arguably, such environments are normalizing measurement and data in ways that are rendering alternative ways of exercising expertise, or even imagining otherwise, extremely difficult (Daliri-Ngametua et al, 2021; Holloway, 2021). To understand how these conditions have been made possible, we must look historically.

Datafication and Teacher Expertise

While scientistic discourses (e.g. psychological, economistic, etc.) have defined and governed education matters for more than fifty years, the 'datafication' of education is creating an entirely new set of conditions and possibilities that are significantly transforming what we know about teachers and teaching, as well as what teachers are expected to know about their practice and students. We will return to some of these questions in the final chapter of the book, but here we look specifically at more recent developments regarding data and data-use in teacher policy and practice. We begin by telling the peculiar story of how an *agriculture statistician* got to define 'good teaching' in the United States, and how his legacy has transformed the meaning of teacher expertise internationally.

What Does an Agriculture Expert Have to Do with Teachers?

In 1982, the Governor of Tennessee, USA, Lamar Alexander proposed a plan to introduce merit-based pay for teachers in his state. Agreeing with the premise of this idea, the governor found an unlikely advocate in Dr William 'Bill' Sanders, a statistical consultant for the Institute of Agricultural Research at the University of Tennessee. Dr Sanders called upon his expertise in *animal science* and *quantitative genetics* to develop a statistical model for measuring the amount of 'value' a teacher adds to (or detracts from) student learning over time (similar to models used for measuring the 'value-add' of agriculture techniques and marketing strategies).

For those not familiar with the practice, 'value-add models' – VAMs – are algorithms designed to (1) predict the amount of growth a student should demonstrate on standardized achievement tests and then (2) compare the predicted with the actual growth to determine the degree to which value was added or detracted to the student's learning over a defined period of time. In the United States, this number is then attributed to the teacher and routinely used to determine the teacher's relative quality, as well as, in some states, things like merit pay, promotion and even in some cases retention or termination (for reviews on VAMs, see Johnson, 2015; Koedel, Mihaly & Rockoff, 2015). As a consequence of President Obama's signature initiative, Race to the Top, many state and local education systems scrambled to develop or purchase their own VAM for holding teachers accountable. This opened a brand new market for non- and for-profit organizations that had the necessary statistical expertise and capacity to meet the growing demands of schools. It is no surprise that such private services were necessary, given that most local education systems did not have the capacity to develop or run their own model. A data-analytics giant, SAS Inc., purchased Dr Sanders' original VAM and quickly became one of the leading, for-profit VAM providers in the United States (Amrein-Beardsley, 2008).

VAMs are used in other countries as well, though not in the same ways. Indeed, while VAMs have been controversial, they've also become more-or-less accepted as an important tool for evaluating 'achievement performance' of students and teachers beyond the United States (see also Bradbury & Roberts-Holmes, 2017). In England, for instance, VAMs have been implemented with a bit more caution regarding teacher accountability (Sorenson, 2016), with VAM output rarely being used for individual teacher appraisal. Unlike the United States, England uses VAM-based algorithms to predict how individual students should perform on standardized tests in secondary school, based on performance data determined in early-years testing (see Bradbury & Roberts-Holmes, 2017). Throughout the student's academic progression through primary and secondary schooling, teachers use this single prediction to determine whether students are tracking towards their ultimate predicted growth expectation, making sure to intervene when necessary. One of us (Holloway) spent time in London recently, interviewing teachers about their experience using data and their perceptions of teacher expertise. Based on discussions with teachers about this practice, it seems as though VAMs have had a significant impact on how teachers see themselves as experts and how the algorithms shape what counts as expertise.

One conversation in particular stands out; it was with a lead teacher – Marsha – who was of the view that statistical predictions are necessary for knowing exactly what a student is capable of achieving. Here is an excerpt from the discussion:

JH: And how exactly do you use the [value-added] data? You said you bring it up before you have meetings with folks and you can look at different targets and whatnot. Are these data used to set the targets; because you said that's one of your big –

Marsha: No, the targets are set from what they get at primary school. It's called the [name of private foundation removed for privacy] and it is a government set formula that they use. And that will mean that we are mainly competitive, I suppose, with other schools. Because if we were just setting our own targets, we would be quite blinkered –

JH: Got it.

Marsha: – whereas if we know the one organisation is setting everybody's nationally, that we are going to stay up there.

JH: I see. Is that target set year to year; or that's set early on and that's what's expected by the time they leave high school?

Marsha: When they leave primary school, they will have a set of data which should determine their pathway all the way up to age 16, in theory.

JH: And how is that navigated; because what if what you find here doesn't gel with what you have learnt from the targets?

Marsha: It is a difficult one. We know students are individuals and they don't always progress at the same linear pace throughout the five years that they are here. We know that some students have a lot of support at home; others don't; they have different struggles. But we also have to acknowledge that those targets are statistically what they can achieve in terms of potential.

JH: Sure.

Marsha: So, we need to have honest conversations, mainly with our teachers, to say, 'Well, look, we know realistically we are just going to have to put intervention in place where we can for this child and just give them what we can; but we can't lose sight of the fact that statistically this is what we should be aiming for.' And that allows us to be consistent with everybody. Because if we were to make adjustment for one student – and we do occasionally, you know, on a case by case basis. If we use our best judgment, we might change some targets. But generally we don't. The way that we can manage that with staff, with parents, with students, is to say, 'Well, look, everybody has the same – we have the same approach for everybody. We can't lose sight of what you should aspire to'.

We can parse this excerpt in a number of ways, but we think it's important to highlight how Marsha prioritizes the statistical prediction for knowing what a student is capable of doing, above and beyond her own experiential and relational knowledge gained through her daily work with students.

It is worth stressing that the above excerpt depicts the *teacher's* perception of teacher expertise and her view that statistical algorithms offer a bias-free assessment of what students can achieve. We find this significant because it demonstrates the power of algorithms and the normalization of quantification in (and out of) education, above and beyond what is oftentimes conveyed in discussions about teachers' use of data. Typically, teacher expertise is framed as something separate from the types of expertise that may influence education. For example, in thinking about the research on the influence of numbers and data in education, we often see calls for teacher expertise to be prioritized over statistics and algorithms. Or perhaps more commonly, for teachers to 'use data' to *inform* their expertise (see e.g. Wyatt-Smith et al, 2021). On the surface, we may agree with this premise. As we've argued in this book, as well as in our respective work previously (see e.g. Gerrard & Farrell, 2014; Holloway, 2021), the capacity for teachers to exercise professional discretion has been undeniably challenged over the past several decades. In large part, this is due to prioritizing metrics and numbers over experiential and relational forms of expertise. However, we also see attempts at framing *teacher expertise* (the construct) as something *separate* from metrics and numbers as drastically oversimplifying the processes through which 'expertise' is made and operationalized. Marsha's reflections above demonstrate that policy challenges around datafication and teachers are not data *versus* expertise, but rather data *becoming* how expertise is understood, exercised and felt by teachers.

Arguably, teacher expertise cannot be separated from numbers and metrics because of how institutional policies, incentives, practices and norms have gradually constructed – and sometimes demanded – expert practice in the image of data (see Daliri-Ngametua, 2021; Lewis & Holloway, 2019; Wescott, forthcoming). The excerpt from Marsha is but one example of how this plays out in practice. Her expertise is her reliance on, and use of, the statistical predictions about her students' capabilities. There are other factors that make up her expertise, of course, but metrics and numbers are central to how she practises as, and understands herself to be, an expert teacher.

To make sense of teacher expertise as being (re)constructed by datafication, we find it useful to think about the material and discursive infrastructures that laid the foundation for such logics, techniques and technologies to emerge. Discourses and technologies – such as datafication – have epistemological and ontological power, shaping what we know, how we know, how that knowledge operates in the world and how worlds are made possible (cf. Foucault, 1980). From this view, datafication is more than technological tools, more than shifts in school foci and more than new policy priorities. While all of these have tangible effects on teacher expertise, datafication also transforms expertise at its core – it has significant epistemic power. This has been made possible through gradually normalizing education as an institution wedded to performance, achievement and the assessment and categorization of students (and increasingly teachers) to meet the needs of modern capitalist societies (Davies & Bansel, 2007; Gee et al, 2019). Thus, we now turn to considering how datafication and the ideas and practices of 'measurement', stemming from economics, have become increasingly understood as necessary for constituting 'good teaching' and identifying 'the good teacher'.

Economic Logics and Techniques in Education

Since the 1970s, the expertise of statisticians (particularly from economics) has been highly influential not only in education but also in most social matters, such as health, social services and transportation, just to name a few (Amrein-Beardsley & Holloway, 2019; Fourcade et al, 2015; Lazear, 1999, 2001; Mau, 2020). In large part, statistical forms of expertise expanded quickly across multiple contexts because of their claims to be neutral and transferable (Gorur, 2018; Porter, 1996). Take, for instance, VAM pioneer and agricultural geneticist Dr Sanders, whose list of accolades range from the modelling of nutrient flow in rivers systems, to developing forecasting systems for Bike Athletic and improving processes for measuring fibre properties. The point of this is to say that Sanders's broad influence must be understood in the rising influence of economics and statisticians more generally. However, while claims to transferability and neutrality may be appealing, they are also the key reasons why the rising significance of economic expertise in fields like education is problematic. Economics boasts a more rigorous approach capable of great generalizations, yet it is the simplification of social matters that constrains the possible contribution of economics to complex social practices (like education). Reflecting on the power and pitfalls of his discipline in 1999, professor of economics, Edward Lazear put it this way:

> It is the ability to abstract that allows us [economists] to answer questions about a complicated world ... I have argued elsewhere that the strength of economic theory is that it is rigorous and analytic. But the weakness of economics is that to be rigorous, simplifying assumptions must be made that constrain the analysis and narrow the focus of the researcher. It is for this reason that the broader thinking sociologist, anthropologist and perhaps psychologist may

be better at identifying issues, but worse at providing answers. Our narrowness allows us to provide concrete solutions, but sometimes prevents us from thinking about the larger features of the problem. This specialization is not a flaw [however, as] much can be learned from other social scientists who observe phenomena that we often overlook.

(pp 5–6)

Lazear's critique of his own field is crucial for understanding the limits of economic thinking within education. Whilst we might not agree with his observation that other disciplines are worse at providing answers, from within the field of economics Lazear highlights how economics has become so problematically influential in understanding, and responding to, social problems. More importantly, it's the prioritization of economic thinking, at the expense of other disciplines, that is so flawed.

Perhaps there is no better example than that of teaching to demonstrate the inherent problems associated with using economic expertise to measure and predict complex social matters. There is nothing about teaching that is simple. From the countless micro-decisions that must be made in real time (notwithstanding the fact that each decision can have significant implications for the emotional and physical wellbeing of students), to the seemingly endless policy changes and expectations that teachers must navigate daily, to the extensive list of stakeholders (e.g. governments, private enterprise, parents, principals, the community) who have considerably vested interests in determining what makes a 'good teacher'.

The moving vignette Thompson and Jones (2021) use to open their article, 'The everyday traumas of neoliberalism in women teachers' bodies: Lived experiences of the teacher who is never good enough' evocatively (and painfully) captures the problem of the datafication and measurement of 'good teaching':

She's under the table again, almost too big for the small space. Tears fall and sobs shake her tight body. I crawl on hands and knees to her, not sure what to do and not sure what has led her here. I decide to just sit in this moment with her, in the pain, to let it all flow out until she is ready to speak. She grasps my hand in desperation then we crawl out from the table together, and she moves her head into my lap. She cries and I cry with her, feeling her pain even though I am unaware of the cause. The rest of the class has returned their focus to math sheets and centers, having lost interest in us and I spend the rest of the time devoted to 'math' with half of my body under a table whispering in a child's ear that she is loved. She is enough. While it seems that what we call 'teaching' has flown out the window, I know I am doing something right and in this moment I feel purpose. I also feel loved. I am enough.

This vignette provocatively illustrates the conflicting responsibilities teachers are asked to navigate in their roles. In each decision, teachers are guided by the expertise(s) they have acquired over time – ranging from how to care for a crying child under a desk, to teaching mathematics lessons (at the same time). The truth is that nothing about a teacher's practice can ever be truly encapsulated into datafied measurement. And if that is the case, then the role and function of these measures are seriously misaligned to the work that teachers do, obfuscating, minimizing and dismissing great swaths of what teachers do, while also cultivating very narrow understandings of success and achievement.

Indeed, research from every corner of the world has shown how economic tools and logics have entirely reshaped our understanding of schooling, including the purpose and approaches we value (Falebella, 2020; Grek, 2009; Lingard, 2011; Taubman, 2010; Ydesen, 2019). Teachers, in particular, have been made subjects of economics, transformed into objects of knowledge that can be measured, compared, evaluated and incentivized to 'do better' and be 'more excellent' (Davies & Bansel, 2007). The negative consequences, of course, have been massive. Teachers have been unfairly fired, curriculum choices have been narrowed, students have been tracked into programmes that are hardly equitable, all in the name of boosting scores on tests (see Berliner, 2011; Hardy, 2019). Some of the most ludicrous scenarios have played out in the United States, where individual teachers are evaluated by VAMs. For instance, Luke Flynt, a Florida teacher who taught middle school gifted students, received a negative VAM score and lost out on bonus salary in 2014 (Strauss, 2015). This was all because several of his students failed to get perfect scores on the state's annual standardized test. This is not an exaggeration. In fact, since VAMs make predictions based on prior test scores, Luke Flynt's already high-achieving students were predicted to score perfectly, or above perfect (literally). Luke (cited in Strauss, 2015, n.p.) appealed his evaluation to the school board, explaining his unbelievable story as follows:

> One of my sixth-grade students had a predicted score of 286.34. However, the highest a sixth-grade student can earn is 283. The student did earn a 283, incidentally. Despite the fact that she earned a perfect score, she counted negatively toward my valuation because she was 3 points below predicted. In total, almost half of the students who counted toward my VAM – 50 of 102 – fell short of their predicted score. That sounds bad. Really, really bad. But a closer look at the numbers is necessary to tell the complete story. Of the 50 students who did not meet their predicted score, 10 percent missed zero or one question, 18 percent missed two or fewer questions, 36 percent missed three or fewer questions, 58 percent missed four or fewer questions. Let me stop to explain the magnitude of missing four or fewer questions. Since the reading FCAT [the test that was given] contained 45 questions, a student who missed four or fewer would have answered at least 90 percent of the questions correctly. That means that 58 percent of the students whose performance negatively affected my evaluation earned at least 90 percent of the possible points on the FCAT. Where is the value in the value-added model? How does all of this data and the enormous amount of time spent testing add value to me as a teacher, to students, to parents or to

the community at large. It leads me to wonder what more can I possibly do, when the state issues predictions for my students that are impossible for them to meet, when I suffer financially because of my students test scores, what more can I do?

Luke's story might seem like an anomaly, but teachers being punished for matters that are beyond their control are common features of such high-stake accountability systems (Berliner, 2018; Collins, 2014). Whether teachers are employed in under-funded and under-resourced schools, or they teach higher concentrations of students with special needs, there are many reasons teachers' evaluations are conditional on their environments, rather than their ability to teach well (Berliner, 2018; Cochran-Smith et al, 2013). As Campbell (2020) importantly reminds us, race is also a significant factor in the evaluation of teachers. Her analysis of teacher evaluation data in North Carolina, USA, found that Black women were rated significantly lower than their white women colleagues.

Unsurprisingly, the conditions of such flawed evaluation systems have led to all sorts of behaviours that might be tempting to call 'bad' teaching practice. These include, for example, things like teaching-to-the test, refusing to teach students who are expected to test poorly, or, in more extreme cases, changing test scores to avoid punishments associated with low test performance. The same year Luke Flynt received his negative VAM evaluation, eleven Atlanta, Georgia teachers were convicted and sentenced to jail for engaging in systematic cheating on the state's annual standardized test (Stark, 2018). While this might be another extreme case, it is worth noting that cheating is made of many shades of grey, and, as Campbell's (1976) Law reminds us, 'the more any quantitative social indicator is used for social decision-making, the more subject it will be to corruption pressures and the more apt it will be to distort and corrupt the social processes it is intended to monitor' (p 49). At the same time, of course, great lengths are taken to control the possibilities of 'cheating', like teachers not being allowed to proctor their own students while taking the annual standardized test (see Garver, 2020). Perhaps if there was more focus on conditions, rather than on the potential for teachers to behave badly, then teachers could focus on developing their expertise for more educative purposes.

Nonetheless, economical thinking has found a home in education policy and practise so much so that many see the 'big dilemma' for teacher expertise as the need for perfecting the calculative tools to more precisely capture the essence of good teaching, relying entirely on the key econometric principle of parsimoniousness. In our view, the very premise of using economic expertise as the primary logic of teacher expertise is absurd. We won't go into further detail about the vast scope of unintended consequences related to high-stakes (and low-stakes) testing, as there is already an extensive literature on this (Amrein-Beardsley et al, 2010; Au, 2010; Nichols & Berliner, 2007). But we do want to make the point that, like anything, expertise is 'corruptible' in the sense that it is shaped by whatever is being asked of it to achieve. This cannot be passed off as a matter of so-called bad morals or a few 'bad apples'. Rather, in an environment where the stakes are so high that it becomes logical to respond in ways that might seem dishonest or immoral, then the expert is, for all intents and purposes, acting rationally. Rather than seeing the expert or their expertise as being problematic, the problem is with the conditions that are structured to elicit such behaviours. This is the case with the teachers in Atlanta, and it also speaks to a broader point about the construct of teacher expertise as being a response to specific conditions and expectations. With the ever-expanding responsibilities that are asked of teachers – which have only increased in the time of Covid-19 – the expertise they are expected to develop and employ in any given moment is always elusive and forever shifting. At the same time, rather ironically, the means to control teacher's expertise continues to tighten, especially as digital technologies open up entirely new ways of doing so.

While 'datafication' broadly is used to signify a rapidly emerging era of schooling that reflects broader movements regarding the 'datafied society' (van Es & Schäfer, 2017; see also Kitchin, 2014), *digital* forms of datafication allow for nearly every aspect of schooling, students, teachers, etc., to be rendered as data to be collected, analysed, surveilled and controlled (Buchanan & McPherson, 2019; Selwyn, 2015; Williamson, 2017). In their recent book, Wyatt-Smith et al (2021) argue that digital forms of datafication (i.e. data that are collected, stored and analysed in digital format) are fundamentally disrupting the very nature and function of schooling and teaching. Building on the material and discursive infrastructures established by economic and data science thinking, digital datafication enables a whole new set of possibilities for monitoring, controlling and constructing teacher expertise. We've mentioned this previously, but it bears repeating that the ubiquity of data and metrics has (re)structured nearly every nook and cranny associated with teacher expertise (Buchanan & McPherson, 2019; Deliri-Ngametua et al, 2021). This has been in large part due to the role that economics has had in shaping our understanding of social life, public institutions and even knowledge.

While teachers have been subjected to hyper-data and accountability conditions for decades, the move to 'digitalization' marks a distinct impact on the teacher, as digital data techniques proliferate our reliance on, access to, and ability to capture more data about teachers and their practise than ever before. Datafication scholars suggest that our fundamental understanding of individual people (in this case, teachers) becomes entangled with these data pictures (Lupton & Williamson, 2017; Selwyn, 2015) insofar as a teacher's data profile begins to supersede the actual teacher as the main site of surveillance and control (Thompson & Cook, 2014). Whether it's the algorithms that operate as 'early warning systems' for predicting where teachers should intervene to keep students on track (see Lewis & Hartong, 2021), or digital platforms where unprecedented amounts of data are stored, analysed and reported (by tech companies) for assessing potential risks and evaluating school performance (see Langman, 2021), digital technologies are (re)shaping the sites where expertise is constructed, and also how it is put to use.

Therefore, what we want to emphasize as we approach the end of the book, is how datafication, right now, serves as a response to the 'risks' intrinsic to teacher expertise. That is, datafication is lauded as the objective, rational and ethical means for guaranteeing that students are educated and assessed fairly and equitably. It is promised to remove human bias and discrimination, producing the utopian schools that operate without 'human error' in judgements about student capability and success; schools that may deliver us from the perils of discrimination. However, as Benjamin (2019) writes about so convincingly in her book *Race after Technology: Abolitionist Tools for the New Jim Code*, 'human judgement and discrimination is not removed but coded in. And that coded inequity makes discrimination easier, faster, and even harder to challenge, because this is not just a racist boss, banker, or shopkeeper [or teacher]' (p 32). Gillborn et al (2018) make a similar argument that statistics' illusion of neutrality can be even more dangerous because people assume that quantitative measures cannot possibly be biased or racist. Heeding this warning, it is critical that we think about how datafication is fundamentally changing expertise. It is not more neutral, or less political. It is susceptible to the same biases and privileged knowledges that make up all forms of expertise.

These practices, made possible via historical discourses and infrastructures, indicate that our understanding and critique of teacher expertise will need to be equally responsive to the shifting features, techniques and logics that define it. That is, as new technologies allow for ever-shifting possibilities, so too must our critical lens be amendable to such rapid change. It is for this exact reason that we chose to spend so much of this book on the political and social conditions that animate expertise. We contend that expertise is not only difficult to define because of its inherent complexities (though this is also true), but more because 'expertise' is always in flux and is always being remade in response to shifting conditions.

Thus, we will use our final chapter as a call for educators to get serious about the political dimension of expertise. Rather than fixate on the specific features of what defines teacher expertise right now, we ask that readers take seriously the notion that expertise is always political. Attempts to critique it from a position of neutrality are thus inadequate for confronting the power dynamics that are always present in expert relations, and which should always be scrutinized.

CHAPTER SIX

The Politics of Expertise

We started this book framing 'expertise' as a keyword (Williams, 1985), as something that is essentially contested, dynamic and socially constructed even when strongly institutionally legitimated and prescribed, as is the case with teacher expertise. Indeed, the institutional investments into – and authorizations of – expertise are one of the key means by which it is contested and through which it changes. However, we do not think that this inevitable dynamism is a reason to shy away from ethical and political questions about what expertise means and how it is practised. This final chapter, therefore, turns explicitly to the politics of expertise and the need for *everyone* with vested interests in education, schooling and teachers to face squarely the politics of expertise, even when this might involve conflict or create discomfort. In opposition to the search for a consensus built upon technocratic visions for expertise (such as in the search for the perfect production and use of data, faultless curriculum implementation, higher professional standards and so on), what is needed is brave engagement in difficult politics.

These difficult politics involve accepting that disagreement is a fundamental part of engaging in essentially contested matters. As put by political theorist Chantelle Mouffe (2011, p 10), 'political questions are not mere technical issues to be solved by experts'. 'Political questions', she contends, 'always involve decisions which require us to make a choice between conflicting alternatives' (2011, p 10). Mouffe's call to embrace disagreement and debate recognizes that decisions about the meanings, practices and institutions of teacher expertise *are political*. Following this, she argues that antagonism 'cannot be made to disappear by simply denying it and wishing it away' (Mouffe, 2016, n.p.). Indeed, the desire to control, ignore or minimize disagreement positions 'expertise' as a problem that can simply be solved through technical reason, rather than a practice that is diverse, fluid and sometimes even violent. It ignores the fact that expertise is always the product of historical, social and political arrangements, power relations and institutions that must be addressed and reckoned with. Working with these ideas, we therefore end this book inviting ongoing debate and discussion: what counts as expertise is something that never will, and never can, be settled. We certainly have not settled it with this book. If anything, we hope we have unsettled it.

Of course, the contestation surrounding what counts as expertise, and who counts as experts, occurs in a multitude of ways from debates in the media to those waged in classrooms, staffrooms, playgrounds, boardrooms, government bureaucracies, university departmental meetings and those in academic journals. Teachers, and teacher-based organizations, such as unions, have long been at the forefront of these contestations. In recent years, for example, strikes across Sydney, Chicago, Chile, Argentina and Kenya (to name just a few) all point to how teachers' industrial issues are professional issues, and thus are questions of the production and enactment of expertise. Indeed, many of these strikes combined, what might be considered traditional 'industrial' issues (e.g. pay and conditions) with issues of the exercise of expertise (e.g. teacher judgement, standardized testing and datafication of teaching). With this in mind, a fundamental underpinning presumption of this book is that teacher expertise cannot be separated from the conditions of teachers' work and the ways that teachers understand their political voice.

Yet a common refrain in education is a plea to get 'politics out' of classrooms. For the politically conservative, for instance, many insist that teachers leave aside politics. This occurs in two key ways. First, is the attempt to deny teachers the right to name and address inequalities and injustices by labelling these as divisive and controversial. Contemporary schooling is characterized by various attempts to silence teachers, for instance, on race and racism and affirming transgender and gender diverse existences. These current-day contestations can be understood as part of a long struggle over the moral character of schooling, its teachers and its students (see Gerrard, 2020). This version of a 'political neutrality' in schools lends itself to forms of expertise that presume that teaching, learning and teacher-student relationships can be understood (and measured) in isolation from the social relations of schooling, and ultimately the diverse lived experiences of students, parents and teachers.

Second is how efforts to standardize and datafy teaching attempt to neutralize teacher expertise, constructing it as a practice that can be nailed down, measured, directed and managed seemingly aside from the messy social relations of the day. We see these moves as seeking to eradicate the underpinning politics of teachers, their work and their expertise. As discussed in Chapter 5, teacher quality and effectiveness have become tools to reshape professional discretion and autonomy, so much so that the idea that teachers might criticize – or even undo – existing social and political stratifications is increasingly absent from the ways policies construct the conditions of possibility for teachers.

In addition, some on the progressive side of politics also attempt to shield teachers from multiple competing political interests by insisting that politicians let teachers' do their work. Here, the concern is that politicians and politics are 'muddying' the work of teachers, denigrating their professional autonomy and disrespecting their expertise. While broadly sympathetic to this view, it is impossible for politicians to be disinterested in teachers. As we noted at the beginning of this book, teachers are some of the most important experts in society. They sit in the nexus between the past, present and future and between states, markets and communities. Teacher expertise is crafted by, and crafts, social values, concerns and relations. It should never be surprising that what teachers do is of interest for all, and ultimately, we should want politicians to be invested in teachers, concerned for teachers to be able to do their work and meet – and advocate for – the needs of their communities.

The attempt to eradicate politics from the work of teaching results in highly technocratic approaches to teacher expertise, as if the work that teachers do can be defined and assessed as a series of attributes and skills. Such an approach presumes it is desirable and possible to bracket society, politics and culture from teacher expertise, teacher education and teachers. The framing of teaching as a set of masterable technical skills and knowledge obfuscates the position of teachers in society, their relationship to governance, and the moral and political dimensions of their practice. Reflecting on the policy moves away from university-based teacher education, Meg Maguire (2014, p 780) suggests there is a 'technology of erasure' when the work of teachers is understood as a set of practical questions that can be answered through school-based training. This erasure narrows teaching such that teachers (and teacher educators) may no longer understand their work as opening possibilities for imagining, working towards and being in the world differently; to imagine the school differently; to imagine the construction and enactment of their expertise differently; to enact their expertise in ways that transcend, trouble and challenge inequalities and injustice. The work, in other words, to enact and engage considerations of equity and justice is more than a set of immediate pedagogic and curricular decisions, but ones that constitute teacher 'expertise' itself. Thus, we need to ask who is the teacher, who is understood to be a teacher, how do they understand themselves as a teacher, and what forms of authority and social agency, status and responsibility do they bring with them?

In reckoning with the politics of expertise, it is necessary to consider the *formation* of experts and expertise. Teacher education is central to the formation of the boundaries that surround who teacher experts are, and what forms of expertise they have. This means that the profession of teachers, and the expertise that teachers are thought to have, is always bounded and thus always exclusionary. At times this has meant the literal exclusion of some from the teaching profession (married women and Indigenous people, to name just two). As we have charted in this book the construction of expertise is a constant interplay of interests in which some things and people get counted, and others do not. What this means is that 'exclusions' in the profession and around expertise are not just things that are 'done to' teachers, but are a part of being and practicing as an expert teacher. Like all knowledge-based practices, there is an inevitable choice about what counts, and what does not count, as expert knowledge and the basis of expert judgement. Understanding what counts and what doesn't is a political deliberation, rather than a technical one. This means, for instance, that attempts to address the exclusions within the profession itself cannot simply be resolved with more and more inclusion that does not alter the state of the profession, or the claims to expertise.

This is poignantly put in Indigenous Lumbee scholar Brayboy and colleague Maughen's (2009) research with Indigenous teacher trainees in the United States. One participant spoke directly to the experience of entering the profession as someone who had experienced first-hand the failure of teachers (and all their so-called collective expert wisdom). Their reflection highlights how 'diversifying' the profession, and thus 'diversifying' the embodied exercise of expertise, must address the political, cultural, economic and social conditions of exclusion:

> I grew up on the reservation. When I was five, my parents decided that I should go to the boarding school for Indians because they thought I could get a good education there.

It was like a military school where the teachers were strict and hit us if we spoke [our tribal language]. I hated it there, but I kept going because I thought education would make a difference. I didn't want the White people in town to call me a 'dirty stinkin' Indian' or think they were better than me. ... I guess I didn't realize that the teachers would also call me a dirty, dumb Indian ... and the education I got was bad anyway and the White people still told me I was dirty and that I stunk. ... That school [the Indian boarding school] could have helped me understand what I know today: My language is a good language and I should know it; I can be smart and Indian at the same time, and I'm not dirty, stinky, or dumb. I can do [many things well] .... I want to be a teacher so that my students can see that being smart and [Indian] can go hand-in-hand.

(2009, p 6)

Commenting on their research, Brayboy and Maughen note they were 'met with great difficulty' in trying to convince fellow teacher educators that what makes a 'good teacher' is not a universality, but will look and feel differently in different contexts and communities, and for different teachers. These are the kinds of political considerations that must be central to teacher education if it is to address the politics of exclusion.

At this point in the book, we think it is also worth cautioning against understandings of expertise that are highly boundaried. While many lament the growing encroachment of non-teacher influence in teacher education and expertise (e.g. policy bureaucrats, edu-capitalists, corporate education 'gurus'), we think the response to this should not be a fortification of the borders of teaching. If anything – as Brayboy and Maughen's research demonstrates – there are some walls of teaching and teachers that still need bulldozing. Thinking with this, we want to challenge the version of fortification that presumes that to have a necessary influence on teacher expertise requires the experience of being a teacher. For instance, the humanities and social sciences – philosophers, ethicists, sociologists, historians and so on – *should* be a part of the professional deliberation in teacher education and in schools about what it means to be a teacher, and what the purpose of teaching is. Moreover, it is essential that many on the 'outside' of the academy, the profession and networks of policy power are also a part of the deliberations: children, young people, parents, communities and community leaders from diverse contexts *should* be a part of the construction of teacher expertise.

Thus, in direct contrast to these attempts to distance teacher expertise from politics, we suggest that teacher education and teachers need to get serious about politics. Teachers spend every day with children and young people, constantly responding to their ever shifting and emerging needs. It is disingenuous (at best) and dangerous (at worst) to presume these daily interactions and decisions can ever be truly neutral. It is impossible, for example, to make a judgement call about ability streaming, anti-racist teaching, the use of high-stakes testing or the need to recognize and respect transgender young people, without an engagement with politics. To be sure, more (or better) data might be able to tell us about the character or extent of inequality, but most often these are not the data points that are currently valued or being produced in teacher education. Moreover, it is not data that tells us what to do. To put it simply: all expert judgements are political ones. This means the challenge is not to try and eradicate politics, or neutralize its effects, but to face it and to consider it a central part of the production and exercise of expertise.

NOTES

CHAPTER 2

1 https://www.independent.co.uk/news/uk/politics/kemi-
   badenoch-black-history-month-white-privilege-black-lives-
   matter-b1189547.html

CHAPTER 3

1 Some aspects of this chapter develops upon the argument
   presented in Gerrard, J. (2022) The educational dynamics of
   populism: Schooling, teacher expertise and popular claims to
   knowledge, *Discourse*.
2 Pamphlet written by the Black Parents Movement and Black
   Students Movement, 1977. Held at the George Padmore
   Archives, London [BEM 3/1/3/7 1–15].

REFERENCES

Allman, P. (2001). *Critical Education against Global Capitalism*. Westport, CT: Bergin and Garvey.

Amrein-Beardsley, A. (2008). Methodological Concerns About the Education Value-Added Assessment System. *Educational Researcher, 37*(2), 65–75. https://doi.org/10.3102/001318 9X08316420

Amrein-Beardsley, A., Berliner, D. C., & Rideau, S. (2010). Cheating in the first, second, and third degree: Educators' responses to high-stakes testing. *Education policy analysis archives, 18*(14), 1–36.

Amrein-Beardsley, A., & Holloway, J. (2019). Value-Added Models for Teacher Evaluation and Accountability: Commonsense Assumptions. *Educational Policy, 33*(3), 516–42. https://doi.org/10.1177/0895904817719519

Andrews, K. (2018). *Back to Black: Retelling the Politics of Black Radicalism for the 21ˢᵗ Century*. London: Zed Books.

Apple, M. W. (1987). Gendered teaching, gendered labor. In Popkewitz, T. (Eds.), *Teacher Education: A Critical Examination of Its Folklore, Theory, and Practice* (pp. 57–83). East Sussex: The Falmer Press.

Apple, M. W. (1996). *Cultural Politics and Education* (Vol. 5). Columbia: Teachers College Press.

Avalos-Bevan, B. (2018). Teacher evaluation in Chile: Highlights and complexities in 13 years of experience. *Teachers and Teaching, 24*(3), 297–311. https://doi.org/10.1080/13540602.20 17.1388228

Au, W. (2010). *Unequal by Design: High-stakes Testing and the Standardization of Inequality*. London: Routledge.

Au, W. (2013). Hiding behind high-stakes testing: Meritocracy, objectivity and inequality in U.S. education. *The International Education Journal: Comparative Perspectives, 12*(2), 7–19.

Bacchi, C. (2000). Policy as discourse: What does it mean? Where does it get us? *Discourse: Studies in the Cultural Politics of Education, 21*(1), 45–57.

Baker, C. N., Peele, H., Daniels, M., Saybe, M., Whalen, K., Overstreet, S., & The New Orleans, T.-I. S. L. C. (2021). The experience of COVID-19 and its impact on teachers' mental health, coping, and teaching. *School Psychology Review*, *50*(4), 491–504. https://doi.org/10.1080/2372966X.2020.1855473

Ball, S. J. (2003). The teacher's soul and the terrors of performativity. *Journal of Education Policy*, *18*(2), 215–28. https://doi.org/10.1080/0268093022000043065

Bascia, N. (2009). Teachers as professionals: Salaries, benefits and unions. In L. J. Saha & A. G. Dworkin (Eds.), *International Handbook of Research on Teachers and Teaching* (pp. 481–9). New York City: Springer US. https://doi.org/10.1007/978-0-387-73317-3_31

Bateman, C. (2022). Nearly half of teachers plan to quit by 2027 due to workload, survey finds. *Sky News*. https://news.sky.com/story/nearly-half-of-teachers-plan-to-quit-by-2027-due-to-workload-survey-finds-12587989

Bishop, M., Vass, G., & Thompson, K. (2021). Decolonising schooling practices through relationality and reciprocity: Embedding local aboriginal perspectives in the classroom. *Pedagogy, Culture & Society*, *29*(2), 193–211.

Beck, S. (2015). The problem of expertise. *European Journal of Pragmatism and American Philosophy*, *VII*(1), Article 1. https://doi.org/10.4000/ejpap.346

BBC. (2017). Michael Gove clarifies stance on experts. *BBC News*. Retrieved 26 November 2021. https://www.bbc.com/news/av/uk-39102847

Beames, J. R., Christensen, H., & Werner-Seidler, A. (2021). School teachers: The forgotten frontline workers of Covid-19. *Australasian Psychiatry*, *29*(4), 420–2. https://doi.org/10.1177/10398562211006145

Benjamin, R. (2019). *Race after Technology: Abolitionist Tools for the New Jim Code*. Cambridge, UK: Polity.

Berliner, D. (2011). Rational responses to high stakes testing: The case of curriculum narrowing and the harm that follows. *Cambridge Journal of Education*, *41*(3), 287–302. https://doi.org/10.1080/0305764X.2011.607151

Berliner, D. C. (2018). Between Scylla and Charybdis: Reflections on and problems associated with the evaluation of teachers in an era of metrification. *Education Policy Analysis Archives*, *26*, 54. https://doi.org/10.14507/epaa.26.3820

Berliner, D. C., & Glass, G. V. (2014). *50 Myths and Lies That Threaten America's Public Schools: The Real Crisis in Education*. Columbia: Teachers College Press.

Bergmann, E. (2018). *Conspiracy & Populism: The Politics of Misinformation*. London: Palgrave Macmillan.

Biesta, G. J. J. (2010). Why 'what works' still won't work: From evidence-based education to value-based education. *Studies in Philosophy and Education*, 29(5), 491–503. https://doi. org/10.1007/s11217-010-9191-x

Biesta, G. (2015). What is education for? On good education, teacher judgement, and educational professionalism. *European Journal of Education*, 50(1), 75–87.

Biesta, G. (2019). Reclaiming teaching for teacher education: Towards a spiral curriculum. *Beijing International Review of Education*, 1(2–3), 259–72. https://doi.org/10.1163/25902539-00102015

Block, D. (2019). *Post-truth and Political Discourse*. London: Palgrave Macmillan.

Bonal, X., & Rambla, X. (2003). Captured by the totally pedagogised society: Teachers and teaching in the knowledge economy. *Globalisation, Societies and Education*, 1(2), 169–84.

Bradbury, A., & Roberts-Holmes, G. (2017). *The Datafication of Primary and Early Years Education: Playing with Numbers*. London: Routledge.

Bragg, S. (2007). 'Student voice' and governmentality: The production of enterprising subjects? *Discourse: Studies in the Cultural Politics of Education*, 28(3), 343–58.

Brass, J., & Holloway, J. (2021). Re-professionalizing teaching: The new professionalism in the United States. *Critical Studies in Education*, 62(4), 519–36. https://doi.org/10.1080/17508487.20 19.1579743

Brayboy, B. M. J., & Maughan, E. (2009). Indigenous Knowledges and the Story of the Bean. *Harvard educational review*, 79(1), 1–21.

Brogberg, G., & Roll-Hansen, N. (2005). *Eugenics and the Welfare State: Norway, Sweden, Denmark, and Finland*. East Lansing: Michigan State University Press.

Browes, N., & K Altinyelken, H. (2021). The instrumentation of test-based accountability in the autonomous dutch system. *Journal of Education Policy*, 36(1), 107–28. https://doi.org/10.10 80/02680939.2019.1689577

Buchanan, R., & McPherson, A. (2019). Teachers and learners in a time of big data. *Journal of Philosophy in Schools, 6*(1), 26–43.

Cabrera, N. L. (2014). Exposing whiteness in higher education: White male college students minimizing racism, claiming victimization, and recreating white supremacy. *Race Ethnicity and Education, 17*(1), 30–55.

Calderon, D. (2014). Uncovering settler grammars in curriculum. *Educational Studies, 50*(4), 313–38.

Campbell, S. L. (2020). Ratings in black and white: A Quantcrit examination of race and gender in teacher evaluation reform. *Race Ethnicity and Education,* 1–19. Advance online publication https://doi.org/10.1080/13613324.2020.1842345

Camphuijsen, M. K., Møller, J., & Skedsmo, G. (2021). Test-based accountability in the Norwegian context: Exploring drivers, expectations and strategies. *Journal of Education Policy, 36*(5), 624–42. https://doi.org/10.1080/02680939.2020.1739337

Carver-Thomas, D., Leung, M., & Burns, D. (2021). *California Teachers and COVID-19: How the Pandemic Is Impacting the Teacher Workforce.* Palo Alto: Learning Policy Institute. https://doi.org/10.54300/987.779

Charney, M., Hagopian, J., & Peterson, B. (Eds.). (2021). *Teacher Unions and Social Justice: Organizing for the Schools and Communities Our Students Deserve.* Milwaukee: Rethinking Schools.

Chatelier, S., & Rudolph, S. (2018). Teacher responsibility: Shifting care from student to (professional) self? *British Journal of Sociology of Education, 39*(1), 1–15.

Chung, J. (2016). The (mis)use of the Finnish teacher education model: 'Policybased evidence-making'? *Educational Research, 58*(2), 207–19.

Churchman, C. W. (1967). Guest editorial. *Management Science, 14*(4), 141–2.

Collins, C. (2014). Houston, we have a problem: Teachers find no value in the SAS education value-added assessment system (EVAAS®). *Education Policy Analysis Archives, 22*(98), 1–42. https://doi.org/10.14507/epaa.v22.1594

Connell, R. (2009). Good teachers on dangerous ground: Towards a new view of teacher quality and professionalism. *Critical Studies in Education, 50*(3), 213–29. https://doi.org/10.1080/17508480902998421

Cochran-Smith, M., Piazza, P., & Power, C. (2013). The politics of accountability: Assessing teacher education in the United States. *The Educational Forum, 77*(1), 6–27. https://doi.org/10.1080/00 131725.2013.739015

Croissant, J. L. (2014). Agnotology: Ignorance and absence or towards a sociology of things that aren't there. *Social Epistemology, 28*(1), 4–25.

Crowther, J., Martin, I., & Shaw, M. (Eds.). (1999). *Popular Education and Social Movements in Scotland Today.* Leicester: The National Organization for Adult Learning.

Daliri-Ngametua, R., Hardy, I., & Creagh, S. (2021). Data, performativity and the erosion of trust in teachers. *Cambridge Journal of Education,* 1–17. https://doi.org/10.1080/030576 4X.2021.2002811

Davies, B., & Bansel, P. (2007). Neoliberalism and education. *International Journal of Qualitative Studies in Education, 20*(3), 247–59. https://doi.org/10.1080/09518390701281751

De Lissovoy, N. (2019). Decoloniality as inversion: Decentring the west in emancipatory theory and pedagogy. *Globalisation, Societies and Education.* 17(4), 419–31. https://doi.org/10.1080/1 4767724.2019.1577719

EdTPA. (n.d.). EdTPA website. Retrieved September 2, 2022, from https://www.edtpa.com/

Elliot, J. (1991). A model of professionalism and its implications for teacher education. *British Educational Research Journal, 17*(4), 309–18.

Ellis, V., Souto-Manning, M., & Turvey, K. (2019). Innovation in teacher education: Towards a critical re-examination. *Journal of Education for Teaching, 45*(1), 2–14. https://doi.org/10.1080/026 07476.2019.1550602

Ellsworth, E. (1989). Why doesn't this feel empowering? Working through the repressive myths of critical pedagogy. *Harvard Educational Review, 59*(3), 297–324.

Evetts, J. (2013). Professionalism: Value and ideology. *Current Sociology, 61*(5–6), 778–96. https://doi. org/10.1177/0011392113479316

Evetts, J. (2018). Professions in turbulent times: Changes, challenges and opportunities. *Sociologia, Problemas e Práticas, 88,* 43–59.

Eyal, G. (2019). *The Crisis of Expertise.* Cambridge: Polity.

Falabella, A. (2020). The ethics of competition: Accountability policy enactment in Chilean schools' everyday life. *Journal of Education Policy*, *35*(1), 23–45. https://doi.org/10.1080/0268093 9.2019.1635272

Fielding, M. (2004). Transformative approaches to student voice: Theoretical underpinnings, recalcitrant realities. *British Educational Research Journal*, *30*(2), 295–311.

Flannery, M. E. (2020). Safety concerns over COVID-19 driving some educators out of the profession | NEA. Retrieved 29 April 2022. https://www.nea.org/advocating-for-change/new-from-nea/safety-concerns-over-covid-19-driving-some-educators-out

Foucault, M. (1980). *Power/Knowledge: Selected Interviews and Other Writings, 1972–1977* (C. Gordon, Ed.; 1st edition). London: Vintage.

Foucault, M. (1983). On the genealogy of ethics: An overview of work in progress. In H. L. Dreyfus & P. Rabinow (Eds.), *Michel Foucault: Beyond Structuralism and Hermeneutics (2nd edition)* (pp. 229–52). Chicago: The University of Chicago Press.

Fourcade, M., Ollion, E., & Algan, Y. (2015). The superiority of economists. *The Journal of Economic Perspectives*, *29*(1), 89–113. doi:10.1257/jep.29.1.89

Frazier, A. (1963). The new teacher and a new kind of supervision. *Educational Leadership*, *21*, 97–100.

Freire, P. (1970). *Pedagogy of the Oppressed*. New York: Herder and Herder.

Gale, T. (2018). What's not to like about RCTs in education? In A. Childs & I. Menter (Eds.), *Mobilising Teacher Researchers: Challenging Educational Inequality* (pp. 207–23). Abingdon: Routledge. ISBN 9781138064607

Garver, R. (2020). Evaluative relationships: Teacher accountability and professional culture. *Journal of Education Policy*, *35*(5), 623–47. https://doi.org/10.1080/02680939.2019.1566972

Gee, J. P., Hull, G., & Lankshear, C. (2019). *The New Work Order: Behind the Language of the New Capitalism*. Milton Park, Abingdon, Oxon: Routledge. https://doi.org/10.4324/9780429496127

Gerrard, J. (2013). Self help and protest: The emergence of black supplementary schooling in England. *Race Ethnicity and Education*, *16*(1), 32–58.

Gerrard, J. (2014). *Radical Childhoods: Schooling and the Struggle for Social Change*. Manchester: Manchester University Press.

Gerrard, J. (2019). The uneducated and the politics of knowing in 'post truth' times: Ranciere, populism and in/equality. *Discourse: Studies in the Cultural Politics of Education*, 42(2), 155–69.

Gerrard, J. (2020). Nationhood, sex and the family: Neoconservatism and the moral dilemmas of privatisation in schooling. In A. Hogan & G. Thompson (Eds.), *Privatisation and Commercialisation in Public Education* (pp. 171–83). New York: Routledge.

Gerrard, J. (2022). The educational dynamics of populism: Schooling, teacher expertise and popular claims to knowledge, *Discourse*.

Gerrard, J., & Farrell, L. (2014). Remaking the professional teacher: Authority and curriculum reform. *Journal of Curriculum Studies*, 46(5), 634–55. https://doi.org/10.1080/0022 0272.2013.854410

Gerrard, J., & Proctor, H. (2021). Activist women, schooling and the rise of grassroots Christian conservatism. *The Australian Educational Researcher*, 1–17. Advance online publication https://doi.org/10.1007/s13384-021-00461-9

Gillborn, D. (2005). Education policy as an act of white supremacy: Whiteness, critical race theory and education reform. *Journal of Education Policy*, 20(4), 485–505.

Gillborn, D., Warmington, P., & Demack, S. (2018). QuantCrit: Education, policy, 'Big Data' and principles for a critical race theory of statistics. *Race Ethnicity and Education*, 21(2), 158–79. https://doi.org/10.1080/13613324.2017.1377417

Gore, J. M. (1993). *The Struggle for Pedagogies: Critical and Feminist Discourses as Regimes of Truth*. New York: Routledge.

Gorur, R. (2018). Escaping numbers? Intimate accounting, informed publics and the uncertain assemblages of authority and non-authority. *Science & Technology Studies*, 31(4).

Grek, S. (2009). Governing by numbers: The PISA 'effect' in Europe. *Journal of Education Policy*, 24(1), 23–37. https://doi.org/10.1080/02680930802412669

Gross, M. (2007). The unknown in process: Dynamic connections of ignorance, non-knowledge and related concepts. *Current Sociology*, 55(5), 742–59.

Groundwater-Smith, S., & Mockler, N. (2016). From data source to co-researchers? Tracing the shift from 'student voice' to student–teacher partnerships in Educational Action Research. *Educational Action Research*, 24(2), 159–76.

Hardy, I. (2015). Education as a 'risky business': Theorising student and teacher learning in complex times. *British Journal of Sociology of Education*, 36(3), 375–94. https://doi.org/10.1080/0 1425692.2013.829746

Hardy, I. (2019). Governing teachers' work and learning through data: Australian insights. *Cambridge Journal of Education*, 49(4), 501–17. https://doi.org/10.1080/0305764X.2018.1557594

Hattie, J. (2008). *Visible Learning: A Synthesis of Over 800 Meta-Analyses Relating to Achievement*. London: Routledge.

Heffernan, A., Bright, D., Kim, M., Longmuir, F., & Magyar, B. (2022). 'I cannot sustain the workload and the emotional toll': Reasons behind Australian teachers' intentions to leave the profession. *Australian Journal of Education*, 66(2), 196–209. https://doi.org/10.1177/00049441221086654

Hogarth, M. D. (2019). Racism, cultural taxation and the role of an indigenous teacher in rural schools. *Australian and International Journal of Rural Education*, 29(1), 45–57.

Holloway, J. (2019). Risky teachers: Mitigating risk through high-stakes teacher evaluation in the USA. *Discourse: Studies in the Cultural Politics of Education*, 40(3), 399–411. https://doi.org/10.1080/01596306.2017.1322938

Holloway, J. (2021). *Metrics, Standards and Alignment in Teacher Policy: Critiquing Fundamentalism and Imagining Pluralism*. Singapore: Springer. https://doi.org/10.1007/978-981-33-4814-1

Hogan, A. (2016). NAPLAN and the role of edu-business: New governance, new privatisations and new partnerships in Australian education policy. *The Australian Educational Reseacher*, 43, 93–110.

Hogan, A., Sellar, S., & Lingard, B. (2016). Commercialising comparison: Pearson puts the TLC in soft capitalism. *Journal of Education Policy*, 31(3), 243–58. https://doi.org/10.1080/026809 39.2015.1112922

hooks, b. (1994). *Teaching to Transgress: Education as the Practice of Freedom*. New York/London: Routledge.

Jackson, J. A. (1970). Professions and professionalization: Editorial introduction. In J. A. Jackson (Ed.), *Professions and Professionlization* (pp. 1–16). London: Cambridge University Press.

Johnson, S. M. (2015). Will VAMS reinforce the walls of the egg-crate school? *Educational Researcher, 44*(2), 117–26. https://doi.org/10.3102/0013189X15573351

Jones, R. (2018). Thinking dangerous thoughts: Post-primary education and eugenics in Australia: 1905–1939. In D. B. Paul, J. Stenhouse, & H. G. Spencer (Eds.), *Eugenics at the Edges of Empire. New Zealand, Australia, Canada and South Africa* (pp. 152–74). London: Palgrave Macmillan.

Kelly, A. H., & McGoey, L. (2018). Facts, power and global evidence: A new empire of truth. *Economy and Society, 47*(1), 1–26.

Kitchin, R. (2014). Big Data, new epistemologies and paradigm shifts. *Big Data & Society, 1*(1), 2053951714528481. https://doi.org/10.1177/2053951714528481

Koedel, C., Mihaly, K., & Rockoff, J. E. (2015). Value-added modeling: A review. *Economics of Education Review, 47,* 180–95. https://doi.org/10.1016/j.econedurev.2015.01.006

Krejsler, J. B. (2013). What works in education and social welfare? A mapping of the evidence discourse and reflections upon consequences for professionals. *Scandinavian Journal of Educational Research, 57*(1), 16–32. https://doi.org/10.1080/00313831.2011.621141

Kumala, V., & Skosana, D. (2014). A history of the South African Democratic Teachers' Union. *South African Democratic Teachers' Union.* https://www.sadtu.org.za/sites/default/files/pubs/history.pdf

Kuranishi, A., & Oyler, C. (2017). I failed the edTPA. *Teacher Education and Special Education: The Journal of the Teacher Education Division of the Council for Exceptional Children, 40,* 088840641773011. https://doi.org/10.1177/0888406417730111

Langman, S. (2021). The power of the platform: Panorama as a producer of (dis)empowerment in educational leadership. *Australian Association for Research in Education Conference,* online.

Larsen, M. A. (2010). Troubling the discourse of teacher centrality: A comparative perspective. *Journal of Education Policy, 25*(2), 207–31. https://doi.org/10.1080/02680930903428622

Lazear, E. P. (1999). *Economic Imperialism.* Boston, MA: National Bureau of Economic Research. Retrieved from http://www.nber.org/papers/w7300.pdf

Lazear, E. P. (2001). Educational production. *The Quarterly Journal of Economics*, *116*, 777–803. doi:10.1162/00335530152466232

Leander, A., & Wæver, O. (2019). Introduction: Assembling exclusive expertise: Knowledge, ignorance and conflict resolution in the Global South. In A. Leander & O. Wæver (Eds.), *Assembling Exclusive Expertise: Knowledge, Ignorance and Conflict Resolution in the Global South* (pp. 1–20). Milton Park: Routledge.

Leonardo, Z. (Ed.). (2009). *Critical Pedagogy and Race*. Hoboken: John Wiley & Sons.

Lewis, S. (2022). An Apple for teacher (education)? Reconstituting teacher professional learning and expertise via the Apple Teacher digital platform. *International Journal of Educational Research*, *115*, 1–14. https://doi.org/10.1016/j.ijer.2022.102034

Lewis, S., & Hartong, S. (2021). New shadow professionals and infrastructures around the datafied school: Topological thinking as an analytical device. *European Educational Research Journal*, Advance online article https://doi.org/10.1177/14749041211007496

Lewis, S., & Holloway, J. (2019). Datafying the teaching 'profession': Remaking the professional teacher in the image of data. *Cambridge Journal of Education*, *49*(1), 35–51. https://doi.org/10.1080/0305764X.2018.1441373

Lewis, S., Savage, G. C., & Holloway, J. (2020). Standards without standardisation? Assembling standards-based reforms in Australian and US schooling. *Journal of Education Policy*, *35*(6), 737–64. https://doi.org/10.1080/02680939.2019.1636140

Lingard, B. (2011). Policy as numbers: Ac/counting for educational research. *The Australian Educational Researcher*, *38*(4), 355–82. https://doi.org/10.1007/s13384-011-0041-9

Lingard, B. (2013). The impact of research on education policy in an era of evidence-based policy. *Critical Studies in Education*, *54*(2), 113–31. https://doi.org/10.1080/17508487.2013.781515

Loughran, J. (2011). What makes a teacher an expert teacher? Monash University News & Events, 23 March 2011. https://www.monash.edu/news/opinions/1784

Lubchenco, J. (2017). Environmental science in a post-truth world. *Frontiers in Ecology and the Environment*, *15*(1), 3.

Lupton, D., & Williamson, B. (2017). The datafied child: The dataveillance of children and implications for their rights. *New Media & Society*, *19*(5), 780–94. https://doi. org/10.1177/1461444816686328

Maguire, M. (2014). Reforming teacher education in England: 'An economy of discourses of truth'. *Journal of Education Policy*, *29*(6), 774–84.

Malewski, E., & Jaramillo, N. (2011). Introduction: Epistemologies of ignorance. In E. Malewski & N. Jaramillo (Eds.), *Epistemologies of Ignorance in Education* (pp. 1–30). Charlotte, NC: Information Age Publishing.

Marom, L. (2019). Under the cloak of professionalism: Covert racism in teacher education. *Race Ethnicity and Education*, *22*(3), 319–37.

Mayes, E. (2020). Student voice in an age of 'security'? *Critical Studies in Education*, *61*(3), 380–97.

Mau, S. (2020). Numbers matter! The society of indicators, scores and ratings. *International Studies in Sociology of Education*, *29*(1–2), 19–37. https://doi.org/10.1080/09620214.2019.1668287

Mayo, M. (2020). *Community-based Learning and Social Movements: Popular Education in a Populist Age*. London: Policy Press.

McGrath-Champ, S., Gavin, M., & Stacey, M. (2019). Strategy and policy: The 'professionalisation' of teaching and the work of an Australian teachers' union. In *Contemporary Issues in Work and Organisations* (pp. 110–26). London: Routledge.

McGoey, L. (2019). *The Unknowers: How Strategic Ignorance Rules the World*. London: Zed Books.

McGoey, L. (2012). Strategic unknowns: Towards a sociology of ignorance. *Economy and Society*, *41*(1), 1–16.

McKnight, L., & Morgan, A. (2019). A broken paradigm? What education needs to learn from evidence-based medicine. *Journal of Education Policy*, *35*(5), 648–64.

McLaren, P. (1998). Revolutionary pedagogy in post-revolutionary times: Rethinking the political economy of critical education. *Educational Theory*, *48*(4), 431–62.

Mede, N. G., & Schäfer, M. S. (2020). Science-related populism: Conceptualizing populist demands toward science. *Public Understanding of Science*, *29*(5), 473–91. https://doi. org/10.1177/0963662520924259

Mills, C. (2007). White ignorance. In S. Sullivan & N. Tuana (Eds.), *Race and Epistemologies of Ignorance (*pp. 11–38*)*. Albany: State University of New York Pr.

Mockler, N. (2015). From surveillance to formation?: A generative approach to teacher 'performance and development' in Australian schools. *Australian Journal of Teacher Education*, 40(9), 117–31. https://doi.org/10.3316/informit.490684795529170

Mockler, N., & Stacey, M. (2021). Evidence of teaching practice in an age of accountability: When what can be counted isn't all that counts. *Oxford Review of Education*, 47(2), 170–88. https://doi.org/10.1080/03054985.2020.1822794

Moodie, N., & Patrick, R. (2017). Settler grammars and the Australian professional standards for teachers. *Asia-Pacific Journal of Teacher Education*, 45(5), 439–54.

Morrison, K. (2001). Randomised controlled trials for evidence-based education: Some problems in judging 'what works.' *Evaluation & Research in Education*, 15(2), 69–83. https://doi.org/10.1080/09500790108666984

Mouffe, C. (2011). *On the Political*. London: Routledge.

Mouffe, C. (2016). Democratic politics and conflict: An agonistic approach. *Política Común*, 9. https://doi.org/10.3998/pc.12322227.0009.011

Mutekwe, E. (2015). Towards an Africa philosophy of education for indigenous knowledge systems in Africa. *Creative Education*, 6(12), 1294–305. DOI: 10.4236/ce.2015.612129

National Commission on Teaching & America's Future. (1997). Doing what matters most: Investing in quality teaching. *National Commission on Teaching and America's Future*. https://www.teachingquality.org/library/doing-what-matters-most-investing-in-quality-teaching/

Newman, J. (1995). Participative governance and the remaking of the public sphere. In J. Newman (Ed.), *Remaking Governance: Peoples, Politics and the Public Sphere* (pp. 119–38). Bristol: Policy Press.

Newman, J., & Clarke, J. (2018). The instabilities of expertise: Remaking knowledge, power and politics in unsettled times. *Innovation: The European Journal of Social Science Research*, 31(1), 40–54.

Nichols, S. L., & Berliner, D. C. (2007). *Collateral Damage: How High-Stakes Testing Corrupts America's Schools*. Cambridge: Harvard Education Press.

Oliveira, A. M. (2021). 'Sterilisation must be done against her will': Coloniality, eugenics and racism in Brazil 2018 – the case of Janaína Quirino. *Australian Feminist Law Journal*, 47(1), 105–22. https://doi.org/10.1080/13200968.2021.1933804

Oplatka, I. (2009). Emotion management and display in teaching: Some ethical and moral considerations in the era of marketization and commercialization. In Schutz, P.A. & Zembylas, M. (Eds.), *Advances in Teacher Emotion Research* (pp. 55–71). Boston, MA: Springer.

Organisation for Economic Co-operation and Development (OECD). (2005). *Teachers matter: Attracting, developing and retaining effective teachers.* Report for the Organisation for Economic Co-operation and Development. Retrieved September 9, 2022. https://www.oecd.org/education/school/34990905.pdf

Ozga, J. T., & Lawn, M. A. (1981). *Teacher Professionalism and Class.* London: Falmer.

Pegoraro, L. (2015). Second-rate victims: The forced sterilization of Indigenous peoples in the USA and Canada. *Settler Colonial Studies*, 5(2), 161–73.

Perryman, J., & Calvert, G. (2020). What motivates people to teach, and why do they leave? Accountability, performativity and teacher retention. *British Journal of Educational Studies*, 68(1), 3–23. https://doi.org/10.1080/00071005.2019.1589417

Picower, B. (2009). The unexamined Whiteness of teaching: How White teachers maintain and enact dominant racial ideologies. *Race Ethnicity and Education*, 12(2), 197–215. https://doi.org/10.1080/13613320902995475

Polly, D., Byker, E., & Putman, S. (2020). Examining elementary education teacher candidates' experiences completing edTPA. *The Teacher Educator*, 55, 1–19. https://doi.org/10.1080/0888773 0.2020.1805535

Porter, T. M. (1996). *Trust in Numbers.* Princeton: Princeton University Press.

Pratt, N. (2016). Neoliberalism and the (internal) marketisation of primary school assessment in England. *British Educational Research Journal*, 42(5), 890–905. https://doi.org/10.1002/berj.3233

Pratt, N., & Alderton, J. (2019). Producing assessment truths: A Foucauldian analysis of teachers' reorganisation of levels in English primary schools. *British Journal of Sociology of Education*, 40(5), 581–97. https://doi.org/10.1080/01425692.20 18.1561245

Rancière, J. (1991). *The Ignorant Schoolmaster: Five Lessons in Intellectual Emancipation*. Redwood: Stanford University Press.

Rittel, H. J., & Webber, M. M. (1973). Dilemmas in the general theory of planning. *Policy Science, 4*, 155–69.

Rizvi, F., & Lingard, B. (2009). *Globalizing Education Policy*. London: Routledge.

Robertson, S. L. (2008). Globalization, education governance, and citizenship regimes: New democratic deficits and social injustices. In Ayers, W., Quinn, T. & Stovall, D. (Eds.), *Handbook of Social Justice in Education*. (pp. 560–71). New York: Routledge.

Rockwell, E. (2011). Popular education and the logics of schooling. *Paedagogica Historica, 47*(1), 33–48.

Rose, N. (1993). Government, authority and expertise in advanced liberalism. *Economy and Society, 22*(3), 283–99. https://doi.org/10.1080/03085149300000019

Rosenblum, N. L., & Muirhead, R. (2020). *A Lot of People Are Saying: The New Conspiracism and the Assault on Democracy*. Princeton: Princeton University Press. https://doi.org/10.1515/9780691204758

Rowe, E. E., & Skourdoumbis, A. (2019). Calling for 'urgent national action to improve the quality of initial teacher education': The reification of evidence and accountability in reform agendas. *Journal of Education Policy, 34*(1), 44–60. https://doi.org/10.1080/02680939.2017.1410577

Sahlberg, P. (2021). Education: The epidemic Australia is failing to control. *Sydney Morning Herald*. Retrieved 26 November 2021. https://www.smh.com.au/education/the-epidemic-australia-is-failing-to-control-20201229-p56qq3.html

Savage, G. C. (2020). *The Quest for Revolution in Australian Schooling Policy*. London: Routledge. https://doi.org/10.4324/9781003141792

Savage, G. C., & Lewis, S. (2018). The phantom national? Assembling national teaching standards in Australia's federal system. *Journal of Education Policy, 33*(1), 118–42. https://doi.org/10.1080/02680939.2017.1325518

Sellar, S., & Lingard, B. (2014). The OECD and the expansion of PISA: New global modes of governance in education. *British Educational Research Journal, 40*(6), 917–36. https://doi.org/10.1002/berj.3120

Selwyn, N. (2015). Data entry: Towards the critical study of digital data and education. *Learning, Media and Technology*, 40(1), 64–82. https://doi.org/10.1080/17439884.2014.921628

Smith, W. C. (2016). *The Global Testing Culture: Shaping Education Policy, Perceptions, and Practice*. Oxford: Symposium Books.

Smith, W. C., & Kubacka, K. (2017). The emphasis of student test scores in teacher appraisal systems. *Education Policy Analysis Archives*, 25(86). https://eric.ed.gov/?id=EJ1157242

Sorensen, T. B. (2016). *Value-added Measurement or Modelling (VAM): Education International Discussion Paper*. Education International.

Sriprakash, A., Rudolph, S., & Gerrard, J. (2022). *Learning Whiteness: Education and the Settler Colonial State*. London: Pluto Press.

Sriprakash, A., Sutoris, P., & Myers, K. (2019). The science of childhood and the pedagogy of the state: Postcolonial development in India, 1950s. *Journal of Historical Sociology*, 32(3), 345–59.

Stacey, M., Talbot, D., Buchanan, J., & Mayer, D. (2020). The development of an Australian teacher performance assessment: Lessons from the international literature. *Asia-Pacific Journal of Teacher Education*, 48(5), 508–19. https://doi.org/10.1080/13598 66X.2019.1669137

Stapleton, J. (1977). The Headmistress must go. *Race Today*, July/August, n.p. [BPM 5/1/5/5]

Stark, L. (10 October 2018). Prison time begins for Atlanta educators convicted in cheating scandal. *Education Week*. https://www.edweek.org/teaching-learning/prison-time-begins-for-atlanta-educators-convicted-in-cheating-scandal/2018/10

Straßheim, H. (2015). Politics and policy expertise: Towards a political epistemology. In Fischer, F., Torgerson, D., Durnová, A. & Orsini, M. (Eds.), *Handbook of Critical Policy Studies* (pp. 319–40). Elgar. Online https://doi.org/10.4337/9781783472352.00026

Strauss, V. (2015). How students with top test scores actually hurt a teacher's evaluation. *The Washington Post*. Retrieved 9 September 2022. https://www.washingtonpost.com/news/answer-sheet/wp/2015/04/01/teacher-how-my-highest-scoring-students-actually-hurt-my-evaluation/

Schwartz, S. (3 February 2021). Lawmakers push to ban '1619 Project' from schools. *Education Week*. https://www.edweek.org/teaching-learning/lawmakers-push-to-ban-1619-project-from-schools/2021/02

Symeonidis, V., & Stromquist, N. P. (2020). Teacher status and the role of teacher unions in the context of new professionalism. *Studia Paedogogica*, 25(2), 23–45

Taubman, P. M. (2010). *Teaching by Numbers: Deconstructing the Discourse of Standards and Accountability in Education*. London: Routledge.

Tenenbaum, J. (Ed.). (1977). *We Have the Strength: A Forum for Self Help Groups Organised by a Steering Committee of Self Help Groups and the Victorian Council of Social Service*. Melbourne: Victorian Council of Social Service.

Tiana Ferrer, A. (2011). The concept of popular education revisited – or what do we talk about when we speak of popular education. *Paedagogica Historica*, 47(1), 15–31.

Thomas, M. A., Rauschenberger, E., & Crawford-Garrett, K. (Eds.). (2020). *Examining Teach for All: International Perspectives on a Growing Global Network*. London: Routledge.

Thompson, C. (2019). The globalized expert: On the dissemination and authorization of evidence-based education. In: Parreira do Amaral M., Steiner-Khamsi G., Thompson C. (Eds.), *Researching the Global Education Industry*. Cham: Palgrave Macmillan.

Thompson, G., & Cook, I. (2014). Manipulating the data: Teaching and NAPLAN in the control society. *Discourse: Studies in the Cultural Politics of Education*, 35(1), 129–42. https://doi.org/10.1080/01596306.2012.739472

Thompson, K., & Jones, S. (2021). The everyday traumas of neoliberalism in women teachers' bodies: Lived experiences of the teacher who is never good enough. *Power and Education*, 13(2), 88–99. https://doi.org/10.1177/17577438211011631

Tuck, E., & Gorlewski, J. (2016). Racist ordering, settler colonialism, and edTPA: A participatory policy analysis. *Educational Policy*, 30(1), 197–217.

Uetricht, M. (2014) *Strike for America: Chicago Teachers against Austerity*. London, New York: Verso.

UNICEF (2020). Teachers: Leading in crisis, reimagining the future. Joint statement from David Edwards, General Secretary, Education International, Guy Ryder, Director-General, International Labour

Organization, Audrey Azoulay, Director-General of UNESCO and Henrietta Fore, Executive Director, UNICEF. Retrieved 9 September 2022. https://www.unicef.org/press-releases/teachers-leading-crisis-reimagining-future

Van Es, K., & Schäfer, M. T. (2017). *The Datafied Society: Studying Culture through Data*. Amsterdam University Press.

Verger, A., Fontdevila, C., & Parcerisa, L. (2019). Reforming governance through policy instruments: How and to what extent standards, tests and accountability in education spread worldwide. *Discourse: Studies in the Cultural Politics of Education, 40*(2), 248–70. https://doi.org/10.1080/01596306.2019.1569882

Verger, A., & Parcerisa, L. (2017). A difficult relationship: Accountability policies and teachers – international evidence and premises for future research. In Akiba, M. & LeTendre, G. K. (Eds.), *International Handbook of Teacher Quality and Policy* (pp. 241–54). New York: Routledge.

Vickers, M. H. (2015). Neglecting the evidence: Are we expecting too much from quality teaching? In H. Proctor, P. Brownlee, & P. Freebody (Eds.), *Controversies in Education: Orthodoxy and Heresy in Policy and Practice* (pp. 81–9). Switzerland: Springer.

Victoria, Z. (2020). Teachers, nurses and supermarket workers the unsung heroes of the COVID-19 pandemic. *SBSNews*, 1 October 2020.

Warmington, P. (2014). *Black British Intellectuals and Education: Multiculturalism's Hidden History*. Milton Park, Abingdon, Oxon: Routledge.

WWC. (n.d.). *Quick Reference Resources About WWC Processes*. Retrieved 26 November 2021. https://ies.ed.gov/ncee/wwc/WhatWeDo

Wescott, S. (forthcoming). Education policy and practice in the post-truth era: Interrogating the evidence-based hegemony. Unpublished Thesis, Monash University.

Wescott, S. (2022). The post-truth tyrannies of an evidence-based hegemony. *Education Policy Analysis Archives, 30*(95), 1–22.

White, J. (2010). Speaking 'over' performativity. *Journal of Educational Administration and History, 42*(3), 275–94. https://doi.org/10.1080/00220620.2010.492960

Whitehead, A. (1929). *Process and Reality: An Essay in Cosmology*. Cambridge: Cambridge University Press.

Wilkins, C. (2011). Professionalism and the post-performative teacher: New teachers reflect on autonomy and accountability in the English school system. *Professional Development in Education, 37*(3), 389–409. https://doi.org/10.1080/19415257. 2010.514204

Williamson, B. (2014). New governing experts in education. Self-learning software, policy labs and transactional pedagogies. In T. Fenwick, E. Mangez, & J. Ozga (Eds.), *Governing Knowledge: Comparison, Knowledge-Based Technologies and Expertise in the Regulation of Education* (pp. 218–31). London: Routledge.

Williamson, B. (2017). *Big data in education: The digital future of learning, policy and practice.* Sage.

Williams, R. (1985). *Keywords: A Vocabulary of Society and Culture, Revised Edition.* Oxford: Oxford University Press.

Wiseman, A. W. (2010). The uses of evidence for educational policymaking: Global contexts and international trends. *Review of Research in Education, 34*(1), 1–24. https://doi.org/10.3102/00 91732X09350472

Wrigley, T. (2018). The power of 'evidence': Reliable science or a set of blunt tools? *British Educational Research Journal, 44*(3), 359–76. https://doi.org/10.1002/berj.3338

Wyatt-Smith, C., Lingard, B., & Heck, E. (2021). *Digital Disruption in Teaching and Testing: Assessments, Big Data, and the Transformation of Schooling.* London & New York: Routledge.

Ydesen, C. (2019). *The OECD's Historical Rise in Education: The Formation of a Global Governing Complex.* London: Palgrave Macmillan.

Zembylas, M. (2005). *Teaching with Emotion: A Postmodern Enactment.* Greenwich, CT: Information Age Publishing.

INDEX